Adobe Creative Suite 2 How-Tos

100 Essential Techniques

D1399020

George Penston

Adobe Press

Adobe Creative Suite 2 How-Tos
100 Essential Techniques

George Penston

This Adobe Press book is published by Peachpit

Peachpit
1249 Eighth Street
Berkeley, CA 94710
510/524-2178
800/283-9444
510/524-2221 (fax)

Peachpit is a division of Pearson Education
For the latest on Adobe Press books, go to
www.adobe.com/adobepress
To report errors, please send a note to errata@peachpit.com

Editor: Becky Morgan
Production Editor: Lupe Edgar
Copyeditor: Anne Marie Walker
Compositor: Melanie Haage
Indexer: Valerie Perry
Cover design: Mimi Heft
Interior design: Mimi Heft

ISBN 0-321-35674-8

9 8 7 6 5 4 3 2 1

Printed and bound in the United States of America

Acknowledgements

I would like to thank the following people who each helped in their own way with the development of the book:

Pam Pfiffner, for her advice and guidance through the years and for thinking I was the right person to author this book. This book wouldn't exist without her. My editor, Becky Morgan and copyeditor Anne Marie Walker who made certain my thoughts translated into intelligible, cohesive words and sentences, along with the rest of the Peachpit editorial and production team who helped with this book.

And of course, I have to thank all of the talented people who produced Adobe Creative Suite 2 and all of the other Adobe software I've admire through the years. Keep it coming.

Damien Newman, who noticed my affinity for all things Adobe years ago and convinced me to share my knowledge with others. And also, his incredibly talented wife, Sara Burgess, for graciously supplying the artwork I used as a basis in a couple of the Live Trace screenshots.

My friends at Twinsparc, Arturo Rodriguez and Nate Steiner for their early feedback on what I was planning to cover in the book. I also want to thank Nate for suggesting the development of a companion website for the book and the willingness to help me get it going.

Last but not least, I must thank my supportive and understanding wife, Zoe, and children, Isabel and Owen, who managed along without me as I worked on the book.

Beyond the Book

If you enjoy the book, please visit my site, Creative Toolbox, for more techniques, tips and tricks, relevant news, commentary, and useful links. This will also be the home of errata for the book, if necessary.

http://www.creative-toolbox.com/

Contents

Foreword

At Adobe, we strive to make our products the best in class. Adobe Photoshop is the standard for image editing, Adobe Illustrator is our world-class illustration program, and Adobe InDesign is surging ahead as a strong leader in the page layout sector. For each of our specialized applications, we spend much of our time making sure that we meet the needs of customers using those products.

However, over time, we realized there needed to be more.

When we released the first version of the Adobe Creative Suite, we not only wanted to make sure we gave our users the feature-rich upgrades they had come to expect from Adobe, but also to enhance the way they work. After meeting with many of our customers, we saw how, in their daily workflows, they often move between Photoshop and Illustrator, between Illustrator, InDesign and Acrobat, or between Photoshop and GoLive. Sometimes these moves were fluid, and other times they were extremely disjointed.

What became clear is that users needed assurance from us that moving from one application to another would be seamless and that their experience of content creation would be efficient. Customers started asking us how to combine all of the Adobe creative products into one workflow: "I want to be able to create a CD cover label using Photoshop and Illustrator—how should I go about it?"

The integration features that make the Creative Suite a total solution are the key to answering questions like this. We live in a changing world of extraordinarily rapid technological advancement. Today, creative professionals who are looking to create compelling content need to be nimble and ready to publish to any type of media. As methods for information and content delivery are changing, Adobe has also made changes to our products to improve cross-product integration and make the creation of that information and content more efficient.

Adobe Creative Suite 2 How-Tos: 100 Essential Techniques will help you to get up to speed quickly with all of the new integration and component features of Adobe Creative Suite 2. Learn about the tight integration of the new Adobe Bridge and Version Cue CS2 versioning utility and how they can help speed up common workflow processes. Learn how you can share common settings for color and PDF across multiple components of the Creative Suite. Understand better how Photoshop CS2 and InDesignCS2 work together, and how working in native file formats can save you time and frustration. Discover helpful shortcuts and nuances that you never knew about Adobe products.

And be nimble and ready to publish any information, at any time, to any type of media.

Ginna Baldassarre
Senior Product Manager, Creative Suite
Adobe Systems Inc.

CHAPTER ONE

Getting Started

Adobe Creative Suite 2 Premium (CS2) not only offers entirely new versions of Photoshop, Illustrator, InDesign, GoLive, and Acrobat Professional, but also introduces Adobe Bridge—a new application specifically designed to help you preview and work with all your CS2 documents. Adobe has also strived to make the integrated versioning and workflow system, Version Cue, more flexible and easier to use. In addition, the suite eliminates a lot of the headaches associated with working with stock photography with the introduction of Adobe Stock Photos.

Getting acquainted with the multitude of new features and tools found in CS2 is enough to make anyone's head spin. With limited time in a day, uncovering new capabilities in your applications is often at the bottom of your priority list. That's where this book comes in. It's intended to help those new to the product suite quickly get up to speed but also includes useful tips and tricks that longtime Adobe software users will appreciate.

This first chapter helps you get your bearings with the new version of the suite. It highlights the fundamental interface elements common in many of the suite's applications and explains the options available to customize them. The brand-new tools, Adobe Bridge and Adobe Stock Photos, are detailed here as well. So let's get started.

#1 Starting with the Welcome Screens

When you first launch any of the main applications in CS2, a Welcome screen appears. These Welcome screens are great launch pads to learn what's new in a particular application or to run through some tutorials. Most Welcome screens also offer quick and easy access for creating new documents or opening existing ones (**Figure 1**).

Bringing Back the Welcome Screen

So you decided to turn off the Welcome screen and now you're missing it. Well that's okay, you can call it back at any time by going to the application menu and selecting Help > Welcome Screen.

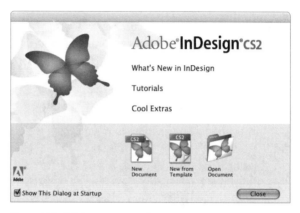

Figure 1 The Welcome screen that opens when you first launch a CS2 application includes links to tutorials, cool extras, and buttons for common tasks.

Although the Welcome screens in Photoshop, Illustrator, InDesign, and GoLive are similar, they do vary slightly in content. Strictly speaking, Acrobat doesn't include a Welcome screen, but it does load a How To window with several links to Acrobat's own help, which explains frequently performed tasks. It's worthwhile exploring each application's Welcome screen to discover what resources and shortcuts to common tasks are available.

As you become more familiar with CS2, the Welcome screens may wear out their welcome. To prevent them from popping up, simply uncheck the Show this dialog at startup check box in the lower-left corner. But don't be too quick to dismiss them. You may be missing out on a good deal of learning resources and shortcuts to common tasks.

#2 Customizing Keyboard Shortcuts

If you find yourself selecting a menu item in a CS2 application several times a day, consider memorizing that menu item's keyboard shortcut. If the menu item doesn't have a shortcut equivalent, you can add your own.

All of the core CS2 applications—Photoshop, Illustrator, InDesign, and GoLive—include a dialog box for customizing its set of keyboard shortcuts (**Figure 2**). You can access an application's keyboard shortcuts dialog by selecting Edit > Keyboard Shortcuts.

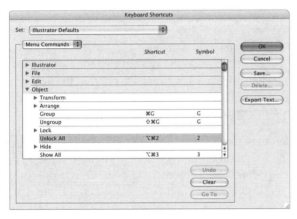

Figure 2 The Keyboard Shortcuts Editor in Illustrator is typical of the type of interface you can expect in a CS2 application to redefine menu and tool shortcut keys.

All the applications include a means for managing your collection of shortcuts, known as shortcut sets, which allow you to create sets for different work modes or keyboards (desktop vs. portables). But before you begin editing an application's shortcuts, it's a good idea to duplicate the default set and work from a copy of it. This way, you'll always have the default keyboard shortcut set to return to.

(continued on next page)

Viewing the Current Set of Keyboard Shortcuts

If you want to view or print out a handy copy of your current set of keyboard shortcuts, click the appropriate button in each application: In Photoshop, click the Summarize button to output a nicely formatted HTML page. In Illustrator, click the Export Text button, and in InDesign the Show Set button to save to a plain text file. Unfortunately, GoLive doesn't offer an export command in its keyboard shortcut dialog.

Each application offers a different shortcut editor to customize its shortcuts. Here's a brief overview of each application's level of customization:

- **Photoshop:** Application menus, palette menus, and tools can be customized via the Shortcuts For menu. The editor is made up of an organized list of menus or tools and their corresponding shortcut, if one is defined.

- **Illustrator:** Menu commands or tools can be customized. Choose the type of shortcut you want from the menu below the Shortcut Set menu.

- **InDesign:** Just about everything in InDesign can be customized. In fact, it offers a very different editor than the other applications. The shortcut types are actually broken out by product area and include a context menu for when you're in a text frame, dialog, and so on.

- **GoLive:** Only menu commands can be customized in GoLive. The editor functions like a pared-down version of the editors found in Photoshop and Illustrator.

#3 Customizing Menus in Photoshop

Photoshop is the definitive "killer app" and with every new version the venerable application amasses a whole new set of features and tools. It's also one of those rare applications that is used in many different ways. All these new features translate into more menus— menus that some users may find valuable but others may never care to see. That's where the ability to customize the appearance of any menu in Photoshop comes in handy. Through a relatively simple editor (**Figure 3a**) you choose which menu items to hide or highlight in color.

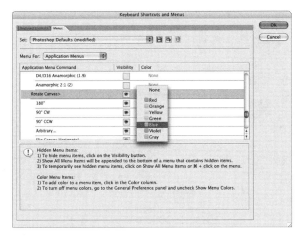

Figure 3a With the Menu Editor, Adobe provides you with total power to customize Photoshop. Now you can decide which menus are visible and even highlight your favorites.

To create a custom menu set, choose Edit > Menus. Choose whether you want to customize the application or palette menus from the Menu For menu. Browse through the list of menus to an item you want to change. To change the visibility of a menu, click the Visibility button to hide a menu, or click the empty Visibility button to show it. To highlight a menu with color, click the None label in the Color column and choose a color. Click either the Save Set button or the Save Set As button to save your settings.

Seeing What's New in Photoshop

Be sure to check out the particularly helpful starter menu set for seeing what's new in Photoshop CS2. Choose Window > Workspace > What's New in CS2 to have Photoshop highlight every menu that directs you to a brand new feature.

Even if you're not quite ready to start customizing your menus, you can still reap the benefits of this great new feature. Adobe includes a handful of starter menu sets that make it easy to see this feature in action. To switch to any of these menu sets, choose Window > Workspace, then select one of the menu sets that appear below Keyboard Shortcuts & Menus (**Figure 3b**). When you're through exploring, you can switch back to the default workspace by choosing Window > Workspace > Default Workspace or choose one of your custom workspaces (see #6).

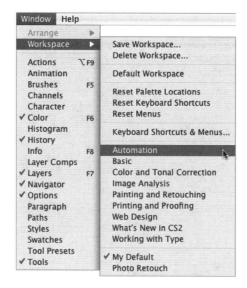

Figure 3b Tucked under the Keyboard Shortcuts & Menus menu are several ready-made menu sets for you to try. They are a perfect way to see Photoshop's menu customization feature in action.

#4 Managing Palettes

No matter how large computer displays get, your workspace still seems to get overrun by all your palettes. Fortunately, several palette management features are found throughout CS2 to keep palettes at bay and your documents in plain view.

To group palettes together, drag one palette's tab into another palette. Grouped palettes can be moved around as a set by dragging the title bar. Palettes can also be docked so they move together but are visible at the same time (**Figure 4a**). Drag a palette to the bottom of another palette to dock it. Individual, grouped, and docked palettes can all be collapsed to just their title bars by clicking the zoom box (Mac) or the minimize/maximize box (Windows).

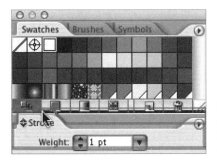

Figure 4a Dock a palette with another by dragging its tab to the bottom of the other palette.

Another great way to manage palettes is to stash them. Stashing palettes collapses them into side tabs where they remain until you click them to slide open (**Figure 4b**). Palette stashing

Figure 4b Palettes stashed to the side of the screen help minimize screen clutter. Clicking the side tab causes the palette to slide out when needed.

(continued on next page)

The Palette Well

The options bar in Photoshop and ImageReady include a palette well for storing palettes you frequently use. Click a palette's tab in the well and it will remain open until you click elsewhere or click the tab again. Drag palettes from their tabs to move them in and out of the well.

is only available in InDesign and GoLive, although Photoshop includes a palette well that behaves similar to stashing. To stash a palette, drag its tab to the left or right side of the screen. To stash a palette group in InDesign, hold down the Option (Mac) or Alt (Windows) key while dragging to the side of the screen. To resize a side tab, drag its bottom edge; to reposition a side tab up or down on the side of the screen, drag the dark gray background behind any tab.

#5 Customizing Toolbars

Although you may be accustomed to the default setup of the Tools palette that's common in CS2 applications, InDesign and GoLive do offer options to change them a bit to complement your work style. This makes it possible to adjust the layout and orientation of some of the tools.

You may value the Tools options available in InDesign whether you're a recent QuarkXPress switcher or just trying to eke out every last piece of screen real estate. Within InDesign access the Preferences dialog. On the General pane, General Options contains the Floating Tools Palette menu (**Figure 5a**). Here you can adjust the Tools palette to be a single vertical column, a standard double column, or a single horizontal row (**Figure 5b**).

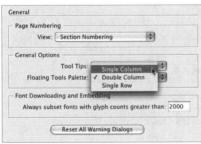

Figure 5a The Floating Tools Palette option in InDesign's General Preferences allows you to lay out its Tools in three different formats. You can even emulate the single column toolbar available in QuarkXPress.

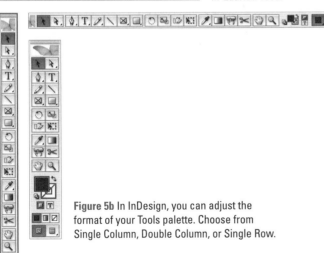

Figure 5b In InDesign, you can adjust the format of your Tools palette. Choose from Single Column, Double Column, or Single Row.

(continued on next page)

Tearing Off Tools

Yet another way you can customize your tools palette is by tearing tools off. Any tool in Illustrator or ImageReady that includes hidden tools can be torn off and made into its own convenient, dedicated tool palette. Hidden tools are additional tools residing underneath the visible tool icon. These are indicated by a small triangle in the lower-right corner of the visible tool. To tear off hidden tools into a separate palette, click and hold on the visible tool and then drag to the arrow at the end of the toolbox and let go. The Pen tool in Illustrator, for example, is ideal for tearing off.

Longtime GoLive users might miss the stand-alone Objects palette now that objects are combined with the Tools palette. You can bring GoLive back to its roots by clicking the Separate tools and objects button located at the bottom of the Tools palette (**Figure 5c**). Click the Join object and tools button found at the end of the separated Objects palette to combine them again.

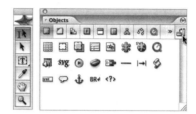

Figure 5c If you want your objects in a standard palette and not part of the Tools palette, click the lower-left icon in the Tools palette to separate the objects from the tools. Once separated, click the icon where it appears in the Objects palette to rejoin the two.

If you want GoLive to only make available the objects allowed in your working markup language, click the Palette Options button, also at the bottom of the Tools palette (**Figure 5d**). Choose Configure and then the markup language you're working with (e.g., XHTML 1.0 Transitional).

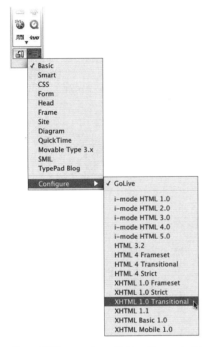

Figure 5d You can have GoLive filter out objects from the Tools palette that aren't valid with your working markup language. Click the Palette Options icon that appears in the lower-right corner of the Tools palette and choose Configure > *your markup language of choice* from the menu to hide the inappropriate objects.

#6 Managing Workspaces

It's not unusual these days to work on multiple computers or work on a computer that's shared with others. This is why a straightforward feature like workspaces, which is common throughout the core CS2 applications, is so useful. You can move your palettes to the locations you prefer and then save that setup as a custom workspace. You can even save multiple workspaces and quickly switch between them to suit your needs.

To create a custom workspace, move and group your palettes to the desired locations, then choose Window > Workspace > Save Workspace (**Figure 6a**). Enter a descriptive name, such as "Photo Retouching" or "Laptop workspace." Now if your palettes inadvertently get moved around, you can quickly get them back to where you like by choosing Window > Workspace and selecting the name of your workspace from the list. All your palettes attentively snap back to where they should be.

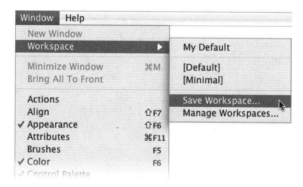

Figure 6a Arrange your palettes to your liking and then choose Save Workspace from the Workspace submenu.

Photoshop also allows you to customize keyboard shortcuts and menu items (see #2 and #3), and link them to your custom workspace. In Photoshop's Save Workspace dialog box, select the options you want to capture—palette locations, keyboard shortcuts, and menus—along with the workspace (**Figure 6b**).

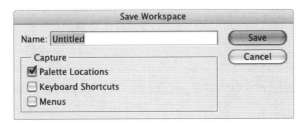

Figure 6b Other CS2 applications allow you to link your palette locations to a workspace. Photoshop takes this a step further by letting you link keyboard shortcuts and menus to a workspace.

If you want to delete a workspace in Photoshop or InDesign, choose Window > Workspace > Delete Workspace. To rename or delete a workspace in Illustrator or GoLive, choose Window > Workspace > Manage Workspaces, click an existing workspace, and then rename or delete it.

Workspaces in Bridge

I already mentioned that workspaces are available in every CS2 application except Acrobat but it's worth noting that the new application, Adobe Bridge (see #7) offers workspaces. Adobe was even thoughtful enough to include four workspaces (with keyboard shortcuts no less) in Bridge to get you going: Lightbox, File Navigator, Metadata Focus, and Filmstrip Focus. Be sure to make good use of them.

#7 Introducing Adobe Bridge

Saving Open Files as File Groups

The Bridge Center lets you save a set of CS2 files as a file group, providing a quick way to reopen all the files in the group. This is great if you have several files you know you'll be working on for a while. To save your open files to a file group, click Save Open Files into a File Group. Whenever you want to open all the files in the group, just select the group and click Open this File Group.

Adobe Bridge is the successor to the File Browser that appeared in previous versions of Photoshop. The File Browser was a virtual light table that made it easy to view and manage your files from within Photoshop. But unlike the File Browser, Bridge is a stand-alone application available on its own as well as from Photoshop, Illustrator, InDesign, and GoLive. Bridge offers much more than just file browsing. It can essentially become the control center for all your projects and a window into all your CS2 content.

Bridge is also meant to be your personal portal into the various support applications and services now offered in the suite. Located as the first option in the Favorites tab, the Bridge Center is a dashboard of sorts where you can view and open recent folders and files, save open files as a group, and read news and tips and tricks related to CS2 (**Figure 7a**).

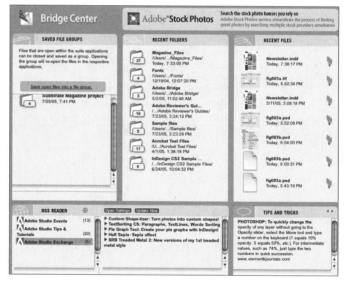

Figure 7a The Bridge Center in Adobe Bridge functions as a dashboard, showing your recent files and providing a place to read CS2-related news and learn new tips and tricks.

Of course Bridge excels at file browsing as well (**Figure 7b**). It can preview all native CS2 files in a myriad of ways (see #12) and lets you drag thumbnails from a Bridge window directly into a layout. Fundamental image management tasks that were once reserved for Photoshop or ImageReady can now be off-loaded to Bridge. You can run batch commands, edit metadata, rotate images, and process images. It can even take over for your operating system's file manager, making it easy to create folders, rename, move, and delete files (see #13). Once you begin working with Bridge, you'll wonder if there's anything it can't do.

Working with Camera Raw Files in Bridge

Bridge supports the Camera Raw plug-in, making it possible to open and edit Camera Raw files directly and then save them in a format Photoshop can work with. Consider this capability in addition to Bridge's built-in automation tools, and it clearly can be your image-processing workhorse while you use Photoshop for more creative endeavors.

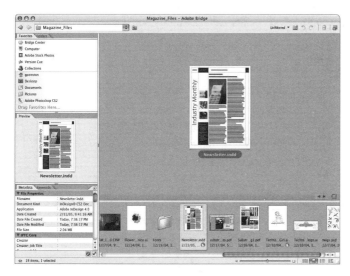

Figure 7b Bridge's file browsing and management features go far beyond the capabilities of the old File Browser. For example, you can now view thumbnails of all CS2-native document formats and work directly with Camera Raw formatted files.

#8 Introducing Adobe Stock Photos

Searching for and managing stock photography has always been a bit of a challenge. You usually have to search across multiple vendors using separate log ins, select the best images, and then download comps for use in your designs. Once your designs are approved, you then have to recount which images came from which vendors, buy the rights for use, and download the high-resolution images to use in your final designs. Adobe saw room for improvement in this process and now offers the Adobe Stock Photos service.

Adobe Stock Photos is available on the Favorites tab in Adobe Bridge (**Figure 8**). With Adobe Stock Photos you can search, view, try, and then buy royalty-free images from various stock photography vendors all in one manageable window and from one account. What makes Adobe Stock Photos even more appealing is that it offers tight integration with all the core CS2 applications. You can download low-resolution comps and easily place them in your designs via Bridge. These comps have metadata associated with them, which is read by Photoshop, Illustrator, InDesign, and GoLive, so they recognize that you're working with stock images even if you rename the files. When your design is finalized, return to Adobe Stock Photos in Bridge to buy and download the high-resolution images used in your design.

Figure 8 Adobe Stock Photos is a welcome feature for those using stock photography in their designs. Its seamless integration within the suite makes the use of stock photography easier than ever before.

#9 Introducing the Help Center

When you have such an integrated suite of applications, you expect a help system that's just as integrated. Well, that's just what Adobe has created. Whereas the original version of Creative Suite had separate help system files for each application that launched in your browser, Creative Suite 2 does away with all this and supplies a single, stand-alone application called Adobe Help Center, which provides help and tutorials for practically every application in CS2.

To launch Help Center from most applications, choose Help > *application name* Help. The one exception is Acrobat, which includes its own help. Once Adobe Help Center is loaded, you can browse the help contents of the currently selected application, search the help by entering terms, or look through the index (**Figure 9**).

Bookmark Your Help

If you find a page in Help Center you'll refer to often, you can bookmark that page by clicking the Bookmark button. Your saved bookmarks appear in the Bookmarks tab located beside the Contents and Index tabs. You can also print the contents of the right pane by clicking the Print button.

Figure 9 The new Help Center is a one-stop shop for all your CS2 information needs. You can search the entire help system or choose a different application from the Help For menu to jump to its specific help contents.

Use the Help For menu to switch to a different application or to search the entire Creative Suite. Supporting applications and services such as Bridge, Stock Photos, and Version Cue are covered in the Creative Suite 2 Help area. There's even help for the Help Center.

#10 Updating Adobe CS2 Automatically

Just as a perfectly tuned car needs scheduled maintenance, Adobe CS2 needs its fair share of periodic updates. Adobe CS2 has a built-in application that automatically checks and updates all the components that make up the suite, much like your operating system software does.

To launch Adobe Updater, choose Help > Updates from any CS2 application except Acrobat. The Updater then checks to see if your Adobe applications need updating. If no updating is needed, a dialog informs you of this. If updating is needed, a dialog box asks if you would like to download the updates (**Figure 10a**). Click the Start Download button to begin the update process. You may be asked to quit some or all of your Adobe applications, so you might want to postpone the update process until you have time to spare. You can click Show Details to see which updates are available and which updates have already been installed.

Figure 10a If updates are available for any of your CS2 applications, this dialog will ask if you want to start downloading them.

You can also configure Adobe Updater to automatically check for updates every month. Launch Adobe Updater, click the Preferences button, and select the topmost check box. You can choose between two options to specify what to do if it finds updates: download all updates automatically and notify you or ask you before downloading any updates (**Figure 10b**). You can then decide which applications to update and specify folders in which to download the updates. Now you'll never have to worry about missing an important update.

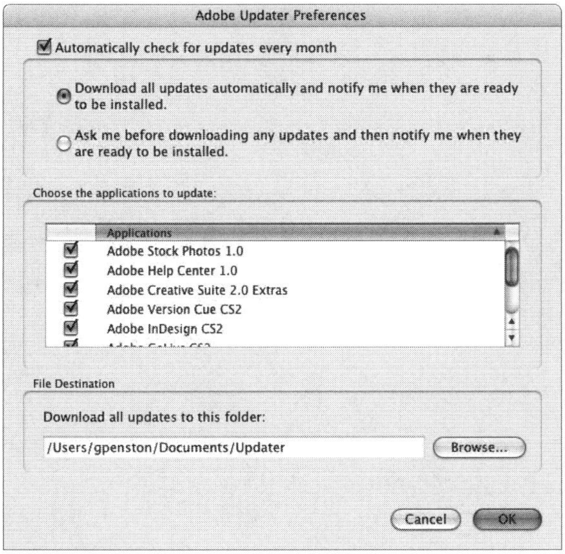

The Product Support Pages

If updating CS2 isn't resolving issues you're experiencing or is causing new ones, go check out the product support/top issues page for the application in question on the Adobe Web site: www.adobe.com/support/. Oftentimes Adobe is aware of the issue and they will post workarounds or information to fix the problem.

Figure 10b Much like your operating system's automatic software updates, Adobe Updater checks for updates every month for you. (If only your car would be as considerate.)

CHAPTER TWO

Working Within the Creative Suite

The Creative Suite's value should really be considered the sum of its parts. Sure, there are the cornerstone applications—Photoshop, Illustrator, InDesign, GoLive, and Acrobat—but look beyond these applications and you'll find the elements that really make CS2 a truly integrated suite: its supporting applications, services, and common user experience.

With the introduction of Bridge, Adobe offers a supporting application designed for browsing and working with visually oriented files. If a picture is worth a thousand words, then Bridge can be your translator. Learning how to work with this new application and discovering what it's capable of is key to working within the suite. Bridge is also the access point into Version Cue CS2, a much-needed, creative-minded, version control system you can quickly set up and start taking advantage of right away.

These supporting tools really go a long way in keeping the suite's components working well together. Although the binding that holds the suite together is its strong support of native file formats and shared user interface elements, learning how all these shared components benefit you when working within the suite is essential.

#11 Accessing Bridge

Adobe designed Bridge to be the nucleus to all of the shared settings, services, and documents you work with within the suite. Although Bridge has a supporting role in the suite, you'll soon consider it indispensable as you start working with it.

So how do you open Bridge? Several options are available to you:

- **Launch the application:** Since Bridge is a stand-alone application, you can launch it just as you would any other application. Add it to the Dock (Mac) or Start menu (Windows) to make it more convenient to access.

- **Click the Bridge button:** The Bridge button 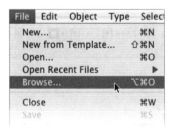 is located at the right end of the Options palette in Photoshop, the Control palette in Illustrator and InDesign, and the Main toolbar in GoLive. Make sure you can see the Adobe Services toolbar in GoLive by choosing Window > Toolbars > Adobe Services Toolbar, which by default is docked to the main toolbar.

- **Use the Browse command:** Photoshop, Illustrator, InDesign, and GoLive also include the menu command File > Browse to launch Bridge (**Figure 11**). The default keyboard shortcut for Browse is Command+Option+O (Mac) or Control+Alt+O (Windows). To remember this shortcut, just think of the common keyboard shortcut for opening files and add Option/Alt to the mix.

Figure 11 Adobe has added the Browse command to almost all File menus in CS2, making Bridge as accessible as opening files.

Automatically Launch Bridge with Photoshop

If you want Bridge to open whenever Photoshop is launched, go to Photoshop's Preferences and select the Automatically Launch Bridge option in the General preference set.

Returning from Bridge

Learning the keyboard shortcut for Browse not only makes it faster to jump to Bridge, but it also helps when you want to return to the application you used to open it. Bridge uses the same default keyboard shortcut of Command+Option+O (Mac) or Control+Alt+O (Windows) for its command for File > Return to {application name}, making it easy to switch between Bridge and the application you're currently working in.

#12 Browsing Files in Bridge

Bridge includes several different views in which to browse your files. You can choose between these views by selecting them from the application's View menu or by clicking their button in the lower-right corner of a Bridge window. Next to the set of View buttons is a thumbnail slider to adjust the size of the thumbnails displayed (**Figure 12a**).

Using Compact Modes

You can switch Bridge to Compact window mode by choosing View > Compact Mode or by clicking the Switch to Compact Mode button in the upper-left corner of the Bridge window. Bridge shrinks down to just the content window in Thumbnails view and floats above all applications. This mode is ideal for dragging files directly into Illustrator or InDesign for placement. While in Compact mode, an Ultra Compact Mode button is available next to the Switch to Full Mode button. Ultra Compact mode still floats the window but hides the content area entirely. To toggle between Compact modes and Full mode using your keyboard, press Command+Return (Mac) or Control+Enter (Windows).

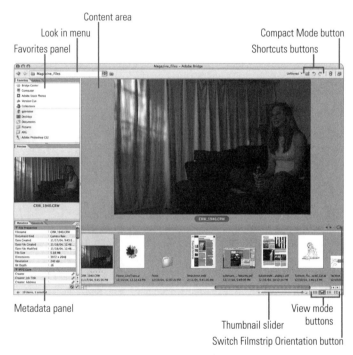

Content area
Look in menu
Favorites panel
Compact Mode button
Shortcuts buttons

CRW_1940.CRW

Metadata panel
Thumbnail slider
Switch Filmstrip Orientation button
View mode buttons

Figure 12a The Bridge window contains several buttons and panels for switching view modes, getting at favorite folders, and editing file details.

(continued on next page)

Create Multiple Windows

Keep in mind that you're not limited to working with just one window in Bridge. Create multiple windows by choosing File > New Window. Then have each window target a different location on your hard drive. You can then drag files between windows to move or copy them to another folder location.

Let's take a look at the various ways you can browse files in Bridge.

- **Thumbnails:** View files in a thumbnail grid.

- **Filmstrip:** View an extra-large thumbnail of the selected file while the other files display as a scrollable list. Click the Switch Filmstrip Orientation button ⟳ to toggle between a horizontal or vertical thumbnail list. An added benefit is that you're able to flip through the pages of a PDF using this view (**Figure 12b**).

    Note You can hide the filename and other details displayed below the thumbnails in Thumbnails and Filmstrip views by choosing View > Show Thumbnail Only.

Figure 12b You can page through Acrobat while in Filmstrip view.

- **Details:** View a scrollable list of thumbnails with useful information, such as color mode, file format, and size displayed beside them.

- **Versions and Alternates:** Similar to the Details view, this view also includes a column displaying any Version Cue versions or alternates of the file if any exist.

- **Slide Show:** Available only from the View menu, Slide Show lets you view extra-large thumbnails using the full screen. Onscreen help appears when you enter this view. You can also switch to Slide Show view by pressing Command+L (Mac) or Control+L (Windows).

#13 Managing Files in Bridge

As you start using Bridge more and more, you may find yourself using your file manager less and less. Sure, Bridge delivers a myriad of ways to browse your files (see #12), but look at some of the ways it can help you manage those files as well.

- **File and folder management:** Create new folders, move, copy and paste, duplicate, rename, and delete folders and files all without ever leaving Bridge. You perform these actions just as you would in your operating system's file manger.

- **Batch Rename:** Your digital camera saves your photos with obscure filenames. Bridge can batch rename them all faster than you can say IMG_2812.JPG. Just choose Tools > Batch Rename (**Figure 13a**).

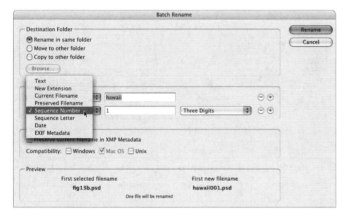

Figure 13a Bridge has its own Batch Rename tool so that you can change the filenames your camera assigns to more human-friendly names.

(continued on next page)

Labeling and Rating Files

Assigning colors or stars to various files is a very efficient way to mark them for future sorting or filtering. Rating and labeling options are located on the Label menu. You can label any selected file with a color (red, yellow, green, blue, and purple), using each as you would a highlighter marker. You can also assign a rating using your keyboard: Command+0–Command+5 (Mac) or Control+0–Control+5 (Windows).

- **View and edit metadata:** Metadata is all the data about the data, such as creation date, file format, author, and so on. Bridge has a Metadata panel (**Figure 13b**) where you can view all this information for a selected file and edit certain properties. A small pencil icon indicates which properties are editable. If you don't see this panel (or any others) on the left side of the Bridge window, click the Show/Hide panels button ◀▶ at the bottom-left corner of the window.

Figure 13b You probably won't frequent the Metadata panel unless you're a dedicated digital photographer, but it's good to know it's there chock full of data about your files.

- **Rating, labeling, and filtering:** Bridge makes it easy to rate and color label files. When thumbnails are selected, a rating control appears below them. Click one of the five dots to assign a rating (**Figure 13c**). Once files are rated or labeled, you can filter them using these attributes. To do so, use the Filter menu next to the New Folder button in the top-right of the Bridge window (**Figure 13d**).

Figure 13c Selecting a thumbnail displays the 5-star rating control. This is also where a color label will appear if you've applied one.

Figure 13d The Filter menu makes it easy to show the highest rated files or those labeled with a certain color.

Drag Folders and Files into Bridge

You can drag folders and files from any location in the Finder (Mac) or Explorer (Windows) to the content area in Bridge to move them into that window's current folder. Mac users can also drag files and folders to the Bridge application icon, and Bridge will open a new window, allowing users to browse the dragged item.

- **Add to Favorites:** If you find yourself navigating often to the same project folders in Bridge, set them up as favorites so they're just a click away. Simply drag any folder, file, or application to the Favorites panel to add it. You can also Control+click (Mac) or right-click (Windows) on them and choose Add to Favorites from the menu.

- **Searching and collections:** You can search for files and folders within Bridge and then save the search criteria as a collection. To start a search, choose File > Find and enter your criteria. Once you run a search, you can save it as a collection so you can run it again another time. Click the Save As Collection button in the top right of the main content area. Saved collections appear in the Collections folder in the Favorites panel.

#14 Synchronizing Color Management Settings

One of the helpful management features in Bridge is its ability to synchronize your color management settings across the suite. Now you can rest easy knowing that your color settings are consistent in all your work.

Note *This feature doesn't guarantee perfect color management—that subject could fill an entire book. It only guarantees that the color settings will be consistently selected in each CS2 application without you having to manually verify them.*

Bridge can automatically synchronize the color settings selected in each application. If the color settings are not synchronized or somehow get out of sync, a warning message appears in any of the applications' Color Settings dialogs. Choose Edit > Color Settings in any of the applications to see whether or not there is an Unsynchronized warning at the top of the dialog (**Figure 14a**). If a warning appears, do the following to remedy the situation:

Figure 14a If you see this warning in a Color Settings dialog, go to Bridge to fix the problem.

1. Go to Bridge and choose Edit > Creative Suite Color Settings (**Figure 14b**).

Figure 14b Bridge ensures that your color settings are synchronized across the CS2 applications so you don't have to.

Sharing Swatches Between Applications

Adobe created a universal swatch format in CS2. This means you can now share color swatches between applications. The colors will appear identical provided your color settings are synchronized. To share a swatch between applications, select Save Swatches For Exchange from the Swatches palette menu and choose a location to save the swatch to. Switch to another application and load the swatch from the Swatch palette menu as you normally would.

2. Select a color setting from the list that best matches your working space. Read through each setting's description to get a better sense of which color setting best suits the media in which you mostly work. Those working with video should select Monitor Color, whereas Web designers would most likely select North America/Web Internet. Print designers should select either North America General Purpose 2 or North America Prepress 2.

If you don't see the color setting you're used to working with, select Show Expanded List of Color Setting Files.

3. Once you've selected a color setting you think best describes your type of work, click Apply. Bridge then synchronizes all the Creative Suite applications with this setting.

#14: Synchronizing Color Management Settings

#15 Setting Up Version Cue

If you asked a group of designers how they normally manage versions of their project documents, you'd probably get a different answer from each. Many probably use different folders or append cryptic number sequences to the ends of their filenames. Version Cue eliminates this file naming madness and makes it possible for a team to work collaboratively on a project without losing their minds.

Version Cue is an integrated version control system available in CS2. But if you look for the Version Cue application, you won't find it, because Version Cue is a service that runs systemwide and works with all CS2 applications.

Note *Version Cue does change the way you work, so it's best to try using it at the beginning of a small project instead of in the middle of a large project with deadlines looming.*

Version Cue is set up for individual use by default. So if you're not planning on using the service with others, you may only need to adjust the Optimize for menu (noted in the following setup). If you want to use Version Cue with a team, you'll need to adjust the workspace settings to allow for project sharing. You'll need to let Version Cue know the size of the team and the type of project you typically work on so Version Cue can adjust its resources accordingly. All of these settings are easily tweaked in the Settings tab of the Version Cue CS2 Preferences:

1. To access Version Cue's settings, select the Version Cue icon and choose Version Cue CS2 Preferences (**Figure 15a**).

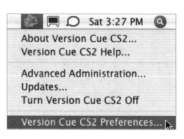

Figure 15a The Version Cue icon provides a shortcut to the Version Cue CS2 System Preference (Mac) or Control Panel (Windows) along with the ability to turn it off and on from this menu.

If you don't see the Version Cue icon, go to System Preferences (Mac) or Control Panel (Windows) and choose Version Cue CS2.

2. To share your Version Cue, from the Settings tab in the Preferences dialog (**Figure 15b**), click the Workspace Access menu and choose This Workspace is Available to Others.

Figure 15b Adjust the controls located in the Version Cue Settings tab so it best suits your working environment.

3. Choose a level from the Workgroup Size menu that best describes your environment on a typical day.

4. From the Optimize for menu, choose an option that best describes the kind of projects you usually work on. If you use InDesign just as much as you use GoLive, leave the setting at Mixed Media. Otherwise, choose Print Media or Web Media.

(continued on next page)

#15: Setting Up Version Cue

Version Cue and Firewalls

If you're having trouble sharing your Version Cue workspace with others, check to see if you're running a firewall. If you are, try disabling it temporarily or opening ports 3703 and 427 and see if that helps.

5. In the Memory Usage field, decide how much memory you want to allocate to Version Cue. If you're running it in a large workgroup or dealing with a lot of files, increase this setting to 256 MB or more.

6. After adjusting the settings, click Apply Now and then choose Restart Now in the dialog that appears. Your Version Cue workspace should now be available to others and ready to use (see #16).

#16 Creating and Working with Version Cue Projects

Once you have Version Cue up and running (see #15), you're almost ready to start working with the service. You'll first need to create a Version Cue project folder in Bridge:

1. Open Bridge (see #11) and choose Tools > Version Cue > New Project.

2. Name your project and optionally add any extra information you'd like to note (**Figure 16a**). If you want to share the project, select the Share this project with others option. Click OK to save your Version Cue project. Now Version Cue is ready to start managing files within the project.

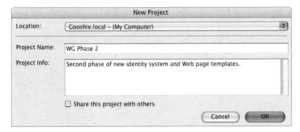

Figure 16a This basic dialog pops up when you create a new Version Cue project. Just enter a name and any extra information, and you're on your way to working with Version Cue.

After creating a Version Cue project folder, you can start using CS2 applications to do any of the following tasks:

- **Add a file:** To add a file to your Version Cue project, choose File > Save As from Photoshop, Illustrator, or InDesign. Click the Use Adobe Dialog button (**Figure 16b**) if you're using the OS dialog box, and then click Version Cue from the Favorites panel (**Figure 16c**). Open your project folder and name your file. Remember, you can now keep your filenames simple since Version Cue will keep track of the versions for you. Add a note in the Version Comments field for your first version and click Save.

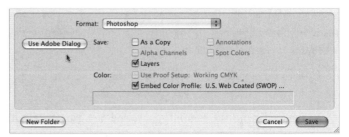

Figure 16b The Use Adobe Dialog button switches from your operating system's standard dialog to Adobe's version.

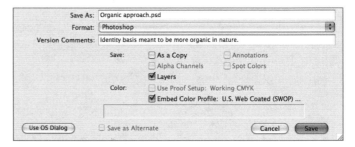

Figure 16c Using the Adobe dialog offers more information about your CS2 documents, including their current Version Cue status.

- **Open and place files:** To open or place files from your Version Cue project, open Bridge and click Version Cue from either the Favorites or Folders panel. Open your project and then open the file you want to work on. Alternatively, you can use the File > Open command using the Adobe dialog.

- **Save a file:** To save a version of a file in Photoshop, Illustrator, and InDesign, choose File > Save A Version. In Bridge, choose Tools > Version Cue > Save A Version. Enter your version comments and click Save (**Figure 16d**).

Figure 16d Being able to add a quick note when creating a new version is helpful, especially when you have to go back a month later and figure out why you changed something and if it was the client or you who decided to make the change.

- **View and manage files:** To view and manage your saved versions, select a file in your project in Bridge and choose File > Versions. The Versions dialog (**Figure 16e**) opens. Here you can view a list of versions of that file and version comments. You can also view, promote, or delete previous versions from this dialog. In addition, you can view and manage versions of a file while it's open in any CS2 application by choosing Versions from the status menu that appears at the bottom of the file window (**Figure 16f**).

Saving Versions of Non-Adobe Files

You can use Bridge to save versions of non-Adobe files such as Word documents or project-related spreadsheets by manually saving or copying your file into your Version Cue workspace. Then be sure to use Bridge to open the file for edits. Make your changes, save your file, and return to Bridge. Choose Tools > Version Cue > Save a Version and enter your comments.

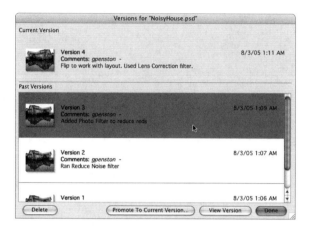

Figure 16e The Versions dialog is where all your versioning diligence pays off. Here you can view your past versions along with a small thumbnail and notes. You can easily promote an older version as the current version as well as view or delete past versions.

Figure 16f You can also access the Versions dialog from the status menu of an open file window.

This tip just touches on the basics of how you can use Version Cue, but it should be enough to determine whether it will work for you or not. If you find Version Cue helpful in your process, be sure to check out Chapter 10, "Working with Versions and Reviews" to learn more about the additional features available in Version Cue and Acrobat.

#17 Appreciating the Control Bars

Regardless of whether you're new to the Creative Suite or just new to this version, you'll come to appreciate the control bars that are now common across the suite. These helpful floating bars serve up a set of controls that are contextually based on the tools and objects you have selected. Control bars prevent you from cluttering your working space with additional palettes just to change a font or precisely adjust the size of an object.

Let's take a look at how each application presents its version of a control bar:

- **Photoshop** calls its bar the options palette (**Figure 17a**). Photoshop also includes a palette well to the side of its control palette for docking palettes you don't necessarily need front and center but want to keep handy.

Figure 17a Photoshop's options palette.

- **Illustrator** now has its own control palette (**Figure 17b**), which offers a unique functionality. Click any control label that appears as a hyperlink and a full version of the palette pops up under the label (**Figure 17c**). Once you click out of the palette, the full palette disappears.

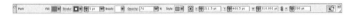

Figure 17b Illustrator's control palette. The most recent addition to the suite.

Figure 17c Labels that appear in blue and underlined in Illustrator's control palette can be clicked to pop up a related palette.

(continued on next page)

- **InDesign** was one of the first CS applications to include a control palette (**Figure 17d**), taking its cue from earlier page layout applications such as QuarkXPress and PageMaker. Although you could probably get pretty far in other applications without using the control bar, I can't imagine attempting this in InDesign.

Figure 17d InDesign's control palette is probably the most robust control palette of the suite.

- **GoLive** distributes the work of a control palette to its two most used palettes: the Main toolbar and the Inspector palette (**Figure 17e**), which is a standard palette that can be stashed (see #4). Be sure to keep both palettes visible so you always have the appropriate options available to you based on what you've selected.

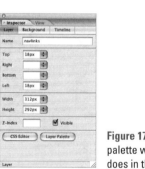

Figure 17e GoLive's Main toolbar and Inspector palette work together to act like a control bar does in the other applications.

#18 Relying on a Common User Interface

One of the advantages of using a suite of applications from the same software developer is that you can rely on a common user interface throughout the product offerings. As the applications in the Creative Suite have matured and become increasingly used in conjunction, Adobe has strived to create a common user experience between them. Menu commands, palettes, keyboard shortcuts, tools, and how you interact with all of these elements have been made more universal wherever possible.

For example, the way you work with opacity settings (**Figure 18**) in Photoshop, Illustrator, and InDesign are in effect the same. The standard Move/Selection tool found throughout the suite uses the same keyboard shortcut (V). And you may have noticed that many of my tips point you to the same menu locations regardless of the application. For example, Keyboard Shortcuts can be found on the Edit menu in every application.

Common Tools for Smarter Working

All of Adobe's hard work in keeping common threads throughout the suite translates into a major productivity boost for you. If you are new to the entire suite or just don't know your way around a couple of the applications, you can take what you learn in one application and use it in another. Armed with this knowledge, you can tread through applications you're not familiar with in the suite with some confidence. If you are quite adept with the pen tool in Illustrator but have never used it in InDesign, it doesn't matter—they're the same. Of course, not every user interface element is common throughout the suite, but so many are.

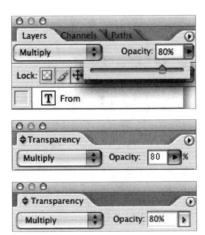

Figure 18 These palettes are used in Photoshop, Illustrator, and InDesign to adjust the opacity setting of an object. They're virtually identical.

#**19** Working with Native File Formats

Back in the early days of Adobe applications, you usually ended up maintaining two separate files when working with different applications: the file in its native format (e.g., .psd or .ai) and the exported file (e.g., .eps) for placing in another application. This resulted in file management headaches that ate up your time and hard drive space. Well, those days are over.

Native file format support across the Creative Suite is something Adobe has been building upon for some time. Now in CS2, you can work directly with each application's file format and take advantage of new integration features by doing so. This is what makes the suite truly shine.

Here are some examples of how applications support the placement of another application's native file format:

- **Photoshop:** Place Illustrator and Acrobat files as dynamically linked Smart Objects (**Figure 19a**).

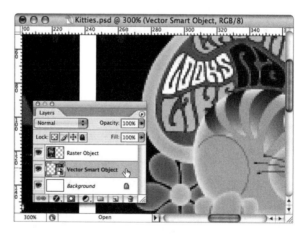

Figure 19a Photoshop not only accepts Illustrator and Acrobat files for placement, but it can now dynamically link them so that it's smart about any updates that are made.

- **Illustrator:** Place or import Photoshop and Acrobat files. Choose a Layer Comp to use when opening Photoshop files (**Figure 19b**).

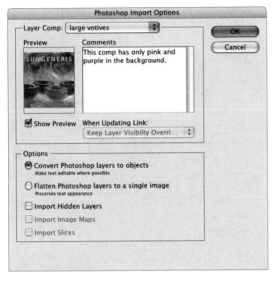

Figure 19b Illustrator has been able to place and import Photoshop and Acrobat files for some time. CS2 now allows you to choose which layer comp to import.

- **InDesign:** Place Photoshop, Illustrator, and Acrobat files. The transparency in a layered Photoshop file is retained (say goodbye to clipping paths). Toggle the visibility of layers in Photoshop and Acrobat files, and switch between different layer comps in a placed Photoshop file (**Figure 19c**).

(continued on next page)

Editing Placed Files

You can easily edit files you've placed in another application and have the placed file automatically update once you save your changes. Select a placed object in Illustrator, InDesign, or GoLive and choose Edit > Edit Original. Or you can Option/Alt+double-click the object to bypass the menu. This opens the linked object in its native application so that you can make your edits. When you're done, save your edits, and when you return to the original application, you'll find the linked file properly updated. No fuss, no muss.

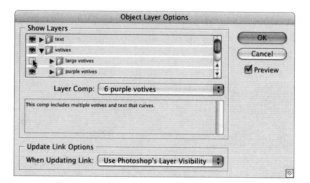

Figure 19c Much like Illustrator's support of Photoshop Layer Comps, InDesign lets you select which comp to use and what layers to turn on without going into Photoshop. That's integration.

- **GoLive:** Place Photoshop, Illustrator, and Acrobat files to create dynamically linked Smart Objects. GoLive creates Web-friendly formats from the native file formats and constantly keeps them in sync.

- **Acrobat:** Although Acrobat doesn't support placement of native file formats, all other CS2 applications are capable of saving files as PDFs. There's no need to print to a PDF or distill files anymore if you're working within the suite.

#20 Sharing PDF Presets

Every main CS2 application is able to save as a PDF file (see #19). So many options are available when creating a PDF that it usually makes sense to use one of the presets available to you and then slightly tweak it if necessary. Using a preset is all well and good, but if you find yourself having to create a PDF in another Creative Suite application, you have to remember which PDF preset you selected and what tweaks you made to it.

The good news is that Adobe has made the Adobe PDF presets dialog virtually identical in every application to make it easy for you to create, edit, and mange your presets. And if that isn't enough, all applications now share the same preset folder location. So if you create a PDF preset in one application, it will magically appear in another.

To define a new PDF preset that's shared among the applications, do the following:

1. Open the Adobe PDF Presets dialog in a CS2 application: In Photoshop, Illustrator, and GoLive, choose Edit > Adobe PDF Presets. In InDesign, choose File > Adobe PDF Presets > Define.

2. Select a preset that you want to base a new preset on and then click New.

3. Adjust the compatibility level and any other settings (**Figure 20a**).

(continued on next page)

Quickly Export from a Preset in InDesign

Once you've established your favorite PDF presets in InDesign, you can use them while skipping the usual Export PDF dialog. Choose File > Adobe PDF Presets > {your favorite presets} while holding down the Shift key. Then all you have to do is name the file and choose a destination. The subsequent Export Adobe PDF dialog is no more.

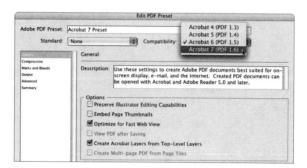

Figure 20a Acrobat PDFs have so many options that it's best to base your preset on an existing one.

4. Enter a name for the preset in the Preset field and click OK. Then click Done in the main preset dialog.

5. Switch to another CS2 application and bring up its PDF Presets dialog. Notice your newly defined preset is immediately available here as well (**Figure 20b**).

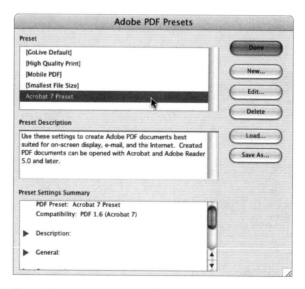

Figure 20b Once you save your PDF preset in one application, you'll be pleasantly surprised to find it ready to use in others.

CHAPTER THREE

Working with Photoshop

There's no question that Photoshop is the crown jewel of the Creative Suite. Through the years, the venerable image-editing tool has become the definitive "killer app." Photoshop is used in so many different ways to accomplish so many different tasks. Graphic designers, digital photographers, and hobbyists can't get far without it. If you're serious about achieving the perfect image, chances are you're using Photoshop.

This powerful, versatile application can be daunting at times. Just when you think you have a handle on the application, a new version arrives with a whole slew of new features and changes. This makes it next to impossible to keep up with it all. A couple of new features are bound to sneak below your radar.

In this chapter, you'll find tips and techniques covering features new to Photoshop CS2 along with some lesser known or frequently overlooked features and tools that have been around for a few versions. In addition, many of the tips in this chapter also work in ImageReady, Photoshop's Web graphics-centric component. Now let's dive deeper into the suite, starting with this image-editing powerhouse and see just what it's capable of.

#21 Making Color Range Selections

Reselecting Your Last Selection

If you find that you need the last selection you made but have since dismissed it, use the handy Reselect command: Select > Reselect. This command loads the very last selection you made no matter how many other actions you've performed since (aside from closing the document).

Efficiently selecting certain pixels to work with while excluding others is essential when working in Photoshop. Fortunately, a number of tools and commands are available to help with this task. One technique you can use to quickly isolate parts of an image is to select them through their similar color range. This works well when you have a consistently colored object set against a differently colored background.

Here are two of the more popular ways to make a selection based on a range of colors:

- **Magic Wand tool:** Clicking in an area that contains relatively similar colors with this tool will immediately select the entire area without having to trace the outside. Experiment with the tool's tolerance and the other settings in the options palette if you're not getting the desired results (**Figure 21a**). A low tolerance value selects colors very similar to one another, whereas a higher value selects a broader range of colors.

Figure 21a If the Magic Wand tool is selecting too little or too much, adjust the tolerance setting in the options bar appropriately. The image on the left shows a selection made with a tolerance of 12, whereas the image on the right has a value of 65.

- **Color Range command:** This powerful command makes it possible to build up a complex selection based on a sampled color range. Follow these steps to use this command:

1. Sample the predominate color you want to create your selection from using the Eyedropper tool and then choose Select > Color Range.

2. In the Color Range dialog (**Figure 21b**) you can adjust the amount of similar colors used in the selection by using the Fuzziness slider.

Figure 21b The Color Range dialog offers an interactive yet sophisticated approach to selecting specific colors in a range.

3. Add or remove colors from the range by using the Add and Subtract from Sample Eyedropper tools and clicking on colors in the image window or preview area.

4. If you want to preview the selection in the image window, choose from the options in the Selection Preview menu.

5. When you're satisfied with the color range selection, click OK to create your selection.

Once you've made your color-based selection, you can clean it up by using the Smooth command. To smooth a selection, choose Select > Modify > Smooth. Enter a value in the Sample Radius and click OK. This will select any nearby stray pixels, resulting in an overall smoother selection.

The Color Replacement Brush

Sometimes you may want to replace the color of an object with another color. The Color Replacement brush, which is tucked under the Brush tool, is just the tool for this. First sample the color you want to end up with using the Eyedropper tool. Then select the Color Replacement brush and start painting over the color you want to replace. In its default sampling behavior, the center of the brush is continuously sampling the color to replace. So be sure to keep the brush within the object's boundaries; otherwise, you'll end up replacing the color outside of the object as well.

#22 Using Layer Masks

If you're making a selection to delete contents from a layer, consider converting the selection to a layer mask instead of permanently discarding it. A layer mask usually starts as a selection that is linked to a layer. The selection acts as a cutout or frame for which only part of the layer's contents show through. The effect is identical to deleting the contents of a layer, but layer masks afford you the freedom to change your mind since the underlying image remains intact. You can always go back and edit the mask.

It's easy to create a layer mask. Make a selection of what you would like to keep visible on a layer (except the Background layer). Click the Add Layer Mask button at the bottom of the Layers palette. Your selection is converted into a layer mask for the selected layer. Notice that a layer mask thumbnail is now linked to your layer thumbnail (**Figure 22a**).

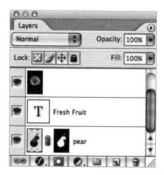

Figure 22a After you create a layer mask on a selected layer, a mask thumbnail appears linked next to the layer thumbnail.

To view just the layer mask, Option/Alt-click the layer mask thumbnail. While in this mode you can edit the layer mask just like any other grayscale image. Areas you paint in white are visible, black are transparent, and anything gray translates into varying levels of transparency (**Figure 22b**). When you're through, click the layer thumbnail to see the effects of the layer mask. If you want to continue editing the layer mask while viewing its effect on the layer, just click the layer mask thumbnail (without the Option/Alt key). If you'd like to move the position of the mask independent of the layer, click the link icon between the layer and layer mask thumbnails. Temporarily toggle a layer mask on and off by Shift-clicking the layer mask thumbnail. To delete a layer mask, drag it to the Delete layer button on the Layers palette.

Figure 22b You can opt to view just the layer mask as you work on it, switch to the layer to see the effects of the mask, or temporarily disable the layer mask to see the layer's actual contents.

Interesting Effects with Layer Masks

Although the simplest method of creating a layer mask is with a selection, just about anything can be used. In fact, many of the popular compositing techniques are based on this knowledge. Try using other images or channels of your image as a layer mask. Also, keep in mind that you can use practically any tool to edit a mask. Apply gradients and filters to achieve some interesting effects within layer masks.

Layer masks are great when you want to use pixels to define your transparent areas, but if you want a hard-edged layer mask with the flexibility of using vector-based tools, you'll want to create a vector mask. You can make a vector mask by creating a work path outline using the Pen or Shape tools. Before you start creating your path, select the Pen or Shape tool and then click the Paths button [▣] in the options bar. After you've created your work path,

(continued on next page)

#22: Using Layer Masks

hold down the Command key (Mac) or Control key (Windows) and click the Add Layer Mask button in the Layers palette. Vector masks work like layer masks, but they're easier to edit. You can even have a layer mask and a vector mask applied to the same layer (**Figure 22c**).

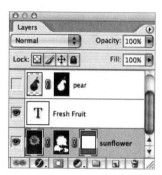

Figure 22c A layer can have a layer mask and a vector mask applied to it at the same time.

#23 Working with Multiple Layers

Ask anyone who's been using Photoshop since its early days what its single most important feature is, and they'll most likely cry out "Layers!" If they're really old school, they can even tell you in which version layers were introduced (3.0). Since the introduction of layers, they've become the foundation of the application. Through the years, many different types of layers have made their way into the application, but how you work with them hasn't really changed much—that is, until now. With CS2, Adobe fundamentally changed the way you work with layers, allowing you to select and control multiple layers at once. Instead of having to explicitly link or group layers just to move them in unison, you can now work with them in a way similar to how you work with them in Illustrator and InDesign. This may not seem like much on the surface, but it can drastically impact your productivity (for better and for worse).

If you've used previous versions of Photoshop, this dramatic shift in how you work with layers may feel clumsy at first. But give it some time, and you'll soon discover the benefits of this new approach. What was once tedious and awkward is now fast and elegant. Here's just some of the ways multiple layer control changes the way you work:

- **Moving and transforming layers:** In order to move or transform multiple layers in previous versions you had to first link them from the Layers palette. Now you simply Shift-click layers in the Layers palette (**Figure 23a**) or use the Move tool directly within the image area (**Figure 23b**).

Selecting Nonadjacent Layers

If you want to select nonadjacent layers in the Layers palette, hold down Command (Mac) or Control (Windows) as you click the layer name. In previous versions, this action would load a selection based on the layer transparency. If you're trying to load the selection, Command-click (Mac) or Control-click (Windows) on the layer thumbnail instead.

Figure 23a It's now possible to select multiple layers in the Layers palette. This simple shift makes tedious layer management a thing of the past.

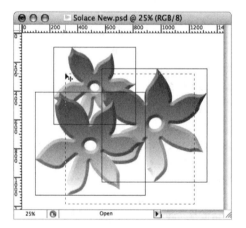

Figure 23b You can now also drag a marquee or Shift-click using the Move tool to select multiple layers directly within the image area. Choose View > Show > Layer Edges to see the bounding box of a layer.

- **Aligning and distributing layers:** This task was so cumbersome in previous versions that many users probably didn't know it was possible. You had to know to first link the layers and then hunt down the menu command. Now whenever you choose the Move tool with multiple layers selected, Align and Distribute buttons are front and center in the options bar (**Figure 23c**).

Figure 23c Although it was possible to align and distribute layers in previous versions, it was a difficult task to manage. Now you're offered these familiar buttons in the options bar whenever you have multiple layers selected using the Move tool.

- **Linking layers:** It's a bit ironic that the multiple layer control makes it effortless to use a feature it essentially makes obsolete. Linking layers is not as necessary as it once was. Now it's just a matter of selecting the layers you want to link and clicking the Link button, which has been relegated to the bottom of the Layers palette (**Figure 23d**).

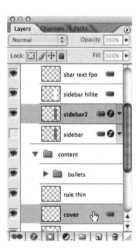

Figure 23d Linking layers isn't as vital as it was in past versions, so it's been reduced to a single button on the bottom, and the link indicators have been moved to the end of the layer row.

- **Grouping layers:** Previously, you had to either link the layers to add them to a Layer Set (now known as a Layer Group) or manually drag them one by one into the folder. In CS2, Shift-click layers and choose Layer > Group Layers or use the standard Group keyboard shortcut: Command+G (Mac)/Control+G (Windows).

Selecting Similar Types of Layers

Multiple layer control also makes it possible for Photoshop to select similar layer types based on your selection. This is useful when, for example, you want to select all the type layers in your document and change dissimilar fonts to the same font. To select similar layer types, select the kind of layer you want to find (image, adjustment, type, fill and shape, or smart object). Next, choose Select > Select Similar Layers. You can then use any commands available to modify the selected set of layers. To deselect all layers, choose Select > Deselect Layers.

#24 Adding Vector Artwork

Although Photoshop is an image-editing application through and through, it's gained a respectable amount of features in the past few versions for working with vector artwork. For instance, you can create shape layers, which are vector-based layers, directly within Photoshop using either the Shape or Pen tools. And if you find these tools a bit limiting, you can create your artwork in Illustrator and then paste it into Photoshop in a variety of ways.

Shape layers

Vector-based shape layers were introduced back in Photoshop 6.0, but you could've easily overlooked them because other features were given the spotlight. That's not to say they don't deserve your attention. Shape layers are an important addition to Photoshop and ImageReady that you should take advantage of whenever possible. They combine the flexibility and resolution independence of vectors with the features available to pixel-based layers, such as blending modes, opacity, and most important, layer styles.

To create a shape layer, choose either the Pen tool 🖊 or one of the Shape tools 🔲 and click the Shapes button 🔲 in the options bar. Draw a closed path with the Pen tool or click and drag with a Shape tool to then create a shape layer. Once it's created, look closely at how the shape layer is represented in the Layers palette (**Figure 24a**). It's really just a fill layer with a vector layer mask (see #22) linked to it. This is useful to know since fill layers can be dynamically changed from a solid color to a gradient, pattern, or an adjustment layer by choosing Layer > Change Layer Content. This level of flexibility makes shape layers ideal for creating interface elements for the Web, which tend to involve several layers of gradients and shading.

Figure 24a Shape layers are really just fill layers with a vector layer mask. They bring the flexibility and control of vector artwork to Photoshop's pixel-based world.

Pasting from Illustrator

Although you can get pretty far using the Pen and Shape tools available in Photoshop to create shape layers, you don't have to stop there. You can also create your artwork in Illustrator, where you have a full cache of tools and filters specific to working with vectors, and then copy and paste it into Photoshop. A dialog appears prior to pasting that prompts you to choose a format for your artwork. Choose from Smart Object, Pixels, Paths, or Shape Layer (**Figure 24b**). If your artwork is relatively simple and you want to continue to edit it directly within Photoshop, choose Shape Layer. If your artwork is rather complex with multiple layers, choose Smart Object (see #25). Both options give you the ability to continue to edit your artwork. The Smart Object format allows you to open the artwork again in Illustrator, whereas the Shape Layer format allows you to edit the artwork using the vector-based tools found in Photoshop.

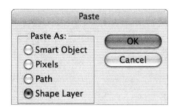

Figure 24b When pasting Illustrator artwork into Photoshop, this dialog appears. Choose Shape Layer for simple artwork you want to continue to work with in Photoshop.

#25 Introducing Smart Objects

Each time you transform a pixel-based object in Photoshop, you degrade the quality of the object to some extent. This is why Adobe included the Free Transform command a while back so that you could scale, rotate, and skew in a single operation. Although the Free Transform command goes a long way toward alleviating the image degradation problem, it doesn't quite solve the problem of multiple transformations. You don't want to worry about the number of times you've transformed an image when you're being creative. Adobe finally solves this problem with the introduction of Smart Objects in Photoshop CS2.

Smart Objects in Photoshop are specially linked objects that dynamically update when the source objects change. The objects can be Photoshop layers or external documents, such as Illustrator, Acrobat, or Camera Raw files. If you've worked with Smart Objects in GoLive, the general concept still holds true. You're free to transform the Smart Object as much as you like without loss of quality since Photoshop dynamically applies the transformations to the linked source file. But Photoshop's approach to Smart Objects differs slightly since they're embedded within the document and represented as a new type of layer called a Smart Object layer (**Figure 25a**).

Figure 25a Smart Objects look and act like any other type of layer. The document icon stamped on the lower right of the layer thumbnail lets you know it's a Smart Object layer.

To create a Smart Object based on a selected set of layers in Photoshop, choose Layer > Smart Objects > Group Into New Smart Object. Placed files are automatically made into Smart Object layers—no matter if they're Illustrator, Acrobat, or other Photoshop files. You can also copy and paste artwork from Illustrator. This is an excellent way to integrate complex Illustrator artwork into

Photoshop. To edit a Smart Object, double-click the Smart Object thumbnail (**Figure 25b**). The embedded object opens in its native application for you to edit. When you save your changes, the Smart Object dynamically updates. As you begin to work with Smart Objects, you'll realize how powerful and innovative they truly are. They will definitely change the way you work in Photoshop for the better.

Note *If copy and pasting artwork from Illustrator doesn't seem to be working, check that both PDF and AICB (No Transparency Support) are selected in the File Handling & Clipboard preferences in Illustrator.*

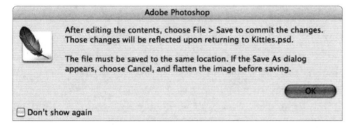

Figure 25b You'll be presented with this dialog the first time you edit a Smart Object. Since working with Smart Objects is completely new, this is actually a good dialog to read through.

#26 Repairing Image Flaws

Repairing in Perspective

Before Photoshop CS2 arrived on the scene, it was rather difficult to repair images with obvious perspective planes, such as the side of a building. CS2 introduces the amazing Vanishing Point filter to effortlessly retouch and paint on images in perspective. To access this filter, choose Filter > Vanishing Point. Next, establish your perspective planes. You can then clone stamp (with healing), paint, and paste content while Photoshop places every adjustment in the correct perspective. Amazing is definitely an understatement.

Photoshop is considered the quintessential tool for retouching and repairing images. It can remove blemishes, crow's feet, and red eye, and re-create missing corners of old photographs as if by magic. And because those magicians at Adobe are continually improving upon the set of retouching tools and filters in Photoshop, it serves you well to know what's new and improved in CS2 for repairing images.

The Healing tools in Photoshop CS2 make it incredibly easy to repair defects in an image. The Healing Brush tool is like the Clone Stamp tool with smarts. You paint from another sampled part of an image, but the Healing Brush blends the painted pixels seamlessly by matching the texture, lighting, shading, and transparency of the pixels being sampled to the pixels being healed. The new Spot Healing Brush makes the retouching process even easier (if that's possible) by automatically sampling the surrounding area being healed. This essentially gives you a one-click retouch tool (**Figure 26a**). Another repair tool that's been made one-click smart is the Red Eye tool. Just click anywhere in the red of the eye with the tool to fix the problem; Photoshop does the rest. It even works on green and white eyes that plague photographs of dogs and cats.

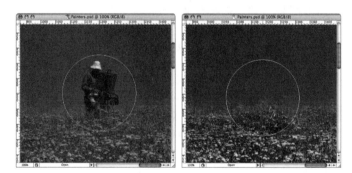

Figure 26a Using the Spot Healing Brush, I was able to remove the painter in one click.

In addition to the assortment of retouch tools Photoshop ships with, it also includes a handful of powerful filters to address overall problems that occur in photographs. For instance, the Lens Correction filter (Filter > Distort > Lens Correction) helps fix common lens flaws (**Figure 26b**), whereas the Reduce Noise filter (Filter > Noise > Reduce Noise) is specifically designed to help remove image noise and JPEG artifacts (**Figure 26c**). If your usual filters for dealing with noise are Despeckle or Dust & Scratches, it's time to give Reduce Noise a try.

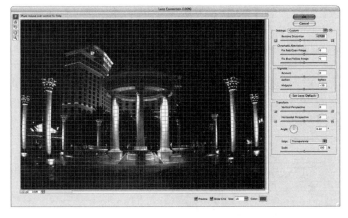

Figure 26b The new Lens Correction filter makes it easy to correct common lens distortion issues such as barrel and pincushion distortion, chromatic aberration, and lens vignetting.

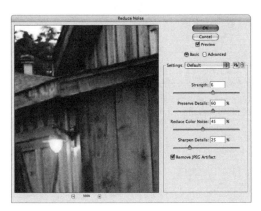

Figure 26c Digital imaging has brought forth such problems as JPEG artifacts, scanned film grain, and overall noise. The Reduce Noise filter eliminates these types of issues as fast as it was to make them.

#26: Repairing Image Flaws

#27 Removing Color Casts

Using Photo Filters

The Photo Filter adjustment layer and command in Photoshop emulates the color filters photographers place in front of their lenses to balance color. To use a Photo Filter adjustment, click the New Fill and Adjustments Layer button at the bottom of the Layers palette and choose Photo Filter. Then select a custom or preset filter option. Warming Filter (85 and LBA) and Cooling Filter (80 and LBB) are useful for tuning the white balance based on color temperature, whereas Warming Filter (81) and Cooling Filter (82) are best for minor color adjustments.

Unfortunately, you can't always count on perfect lighting when shooting your photos. And less than ideal lighting conditions usually result in an unfavorable amount of one color throughout your pictures. This unpleasant effect is known as a color cast. Thankfully, removing these color casts is something Photoshop can do in its sleep.

To remove an undesirable color cast from a photograph, choose Image > Adjustments > Auto Color. Photoshop analyzes the shadows, midtones, and highlights and then automatically adjusts the contrast and color of the image. Sure, you could do much of this yourself via the Levels or Curves commands, but Photoshop does surprisingly well on its own. However, if you feel the result could stand a little help, Photoshop obliges by offering an Auto Correction Options dialog (**Figure 27**). Here you can adjust the settings Photoshop uses when running any Auto Correction commands, such as Auto Color or Auto Contrast. To access these settings, click Options in the Levels dialog (Image > Adjustments > Levels).

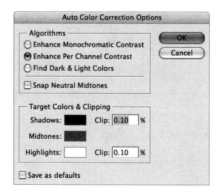

Figure 27 The Auto Color command does a fine job of removing color casts. But if you'd like to tweak the settings, use this dialog.

#28 Using the Smart Sharpen Filter

The Unsharp Mask filter has been the ultimate tool many of us reach for to bring clarity and crispness to our images. With Photoshop CS2, the new Smart Sharpen filter gives the old standard a run for its money. This filter can produce some remarkable results, especially in comparison to what we're used to seeing from the Unsharp Mask filter. This is understandable though, considering that Smart Sharpen offers more controls to adjust how the sharpening is applied and where it occurs.

Give the filter a try to get a sense of how it measures up to the classic Unsharp Mask filter. Open an image and view it at Actual Pixels (100%) to get an accurate view of the sharpening effect. Choose Filter > Sharpen > Smart Sharpen. Notice that the filter offers Basic and Advanced modes in the dialog. Even in the Basic mode it includes more options than the Unsharp Mask filter. Both tools offer Amount and Radius settings, but the Smart Sharpen filter includes a Remove menu to choose the type of blur to remove: Gaussian, Lens, or Motion (**Figure 28a**):

Fix Sharpening Color Shifts

Sometimes when you sharpen a brightly colored image, the colors will shift or become oversaturated. To overcome this problem, choose Edit > Fade sharpen filter immediately after applying the sharpen filter. Then select Luminosity from the Mode menu. This should eliminate the color from shifting.

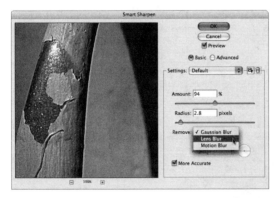

Figure 28a The Smart Sharpen filter includes a Basic and Advanced mode. It also lets you choose between three types of blur removal options.

- Leaving the Remove option on Gaussian Blur gives you results similar to the Unsharp Mask filter.

(continued on next page)

Sharpening with the High Pass Filter

Here's a completely different sharpening technique that doesn't even use a sharpening filter. Duplicate the layer you want to sharpen (Layer > New > Layer via Copy). Then choose Filter > Other > High Pass, select a radius amount (somewhere between 3 and 7 is a good start), and click OK. Now change the layer's blending mode to Overlay, Soft Light, or Hard Light. You can then adjust the layer's opacity to control the amount of sharpening. Although some argue that this technique yields better results than applying a sharpening filter, it's still highly debatable as to which is really better. I suggest trying each and judge for yourself which one works best.

- Lens Blur is a bit more refined, allowing you to increase your Amount value before noticeable halos appear. A halo effect occurs around the edges of an image when oversharpening an image. Keeping halos in check is the fine art of sharpening.

- The Motion Blur option is ideal when your shot has a slight blur because the object or the camera moved slightly. The key is to find the best angle of the blur for the filter to work its magic.

The More Accurate option runs the filter in two passes. This is similar to the technique many users employ of running a weak Unsharp Mask filter twice instead of running a strong one once. I suggest leaving this option on unless you're working with an image with a lot of grain or compression artifacts. This option actually runs the filter twice so it will take longer, but it's worth the wait.

Selecting the Advanced mode makes available the Shadow and Highlight tabs (**Figure 28b**). These tabs allow you to selectively control the amount of sharpening that occurs in the light and dark areas of your image, providing you with independent controls to reduce halos in just these areas.

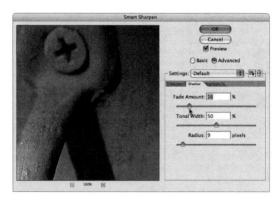

Figure 28b For even greater control on how the sharpening filter is applied, switch to the Advanced mode. Here you can separately adjust the shadow and highlight settings.

#29 Exploring Filter Combinations

If you're experimenting with an assortment of filters in Photoshop, trying to find just the right filter to do the trick, you may be inadvertently limiting your search. Perhaps the effect you're looking for isn't actually the result of a single filter but a combination of filters applied in a certain order. So let me direct your attention to the Filter Gallery.

The Filter Gallery is one of those nice gems like the File Browser that was carried over from Photoshop Elements. This tool allows you to selectively audition filter effects in Photoshop in any combination or order. Once you've discovered the winning combination, Photoshop applies the filters all at once to your image. This potentially could provide you with a higher-quality result than if you applied the filters over time.

Note *The Filter Gallery is also available in ImageReady and Illustrator.*

To use the Filter Gallery, choose Filter > Filter Gallery. The filter opens a window that fills your screen with a large preview on the left (**Figure 29a**).

Figure 29a The Filter Gallery is your one-stop shop for exploring several filter effect combinations at once.

(continued on next page)

Faster Filter Gallery

The Filter Gallery is a great tool for exploring and applying several filter effects at once to your image. But working with an overly large file can make experimenting with the Filter Gallery slow to a crawl. Try selecting a small portion of your image that's representative of the entire image. Once you're satisfied with the effects in the Filter Gallery, click OK to apply them to the selection. If you're happy with the effects applied to the selection, undo the filter, Deselect (Select > Deselect), and reapply the Filter Gallery to the entire image layer. To run the most recent filter again sans dialog, press Command+F (Mac) or Control+F (Windows).

To the right of this is a folder listing of the available effect categories. Expand any of these folders to view the set of filters along with thumbnails illustrating each filter's effect. Click a filter thumbnail to preview its effect on your image. The settings for the selected filter will display in the top right of the window. To apply another filter on top of this filter, click the New Effect Layer button [icon] located in the bottom right of the window, and then select another effect. For a faster method, hold down Option/Alt as you select subsequent effects. As your effects get layered on one another, you can reorder them by dragging them in the effects layer panel (**Figure 29b**). Changing the order of the filters can really impact the overall effect. In the effects layer panel you can toggle an effect on and off, select them to apply a different effect in their place, or eliminate them by clicking the Delete Effect button [icon]. When you're happy with your combination of filter effects, click OK to have Photoshop apply them all at once.

Figure 29b The effects layer panel lets you reorder your effects to see in the preview panel just how each effect interacts with another.

#30 Weighted Optimization for the Web

When optimizing images for the Web, you may think you can only control the compression setting of the entire image slice. But it's actually possible to have Photoshop and ImageReady apply less compression on elements within a slice that may be of importance to you, such as a company logo or type. This accommodating feature is called weighted optimization.

Weighted optimization allows you to use Text or Shape layers (see #24), or pixel-based alpha channels in your document to set a different quality range than that in the overall optimization settings. This makes it possible to apply an aggressive amount of compression on a background while maintaining readability of your crisp type overlay (**Figure 30a**).

Figure 30a Weighted optimization is helpful when you want to reduce the file size without losing image quality in critical areas such as type or a logo.

To take advantage of weighted optimization, do the following:

1. Make sure you have a type layer, shape layer, or alpha channel in your document. Alpha channels are saved selections; just make a selection and choose Select > Save Selection in either Photoshop or ImageReady.

(continued on next page)

Selective Masking with Alpha Channels

When using alpha channels for weighted optimization, remember that alpha channels don't necessarily have to be continuous areas of black and white. If you'd like to get more selective with your alpha channels, edit them directly by selecting them from the Channels palette in Photoshop (ImageReady doesn't have this palette). With the channel selected, you can use any of the tools to paint it however you want. For example, use the Gradient tool to make a linear range for your weighted optimization.

2. In the Optimize panel in Photoshop or the Optimize palette in ImageReady, click the Mask button ☑ next to the setting you'd like to weigh in on.

You'll see different options depending on the format of your image. JPEG format lets you modify the quality setting, whereas GIF format offers optimization mask settings for color reduction, dithering, and lossiness (**Figure 30b**). PNG-8 format allows for color reduction and dithering settings.

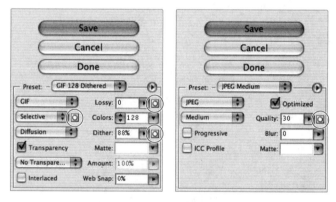

Figure 30b These little mask icons are cues to which settings allow weighting. Really, how could you miss them?

3. In the Modify Quality Setting dialog, choose which masks to modify the compression on: All Text Layers, All Vector Shape Layers, or an alpha channel (**Figure 30c**).

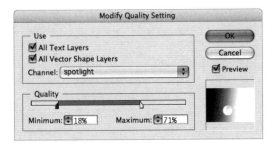

Figure 30c The weighted optimization dialog allows you to give quality precedence to type and shape layers along with an alpha channel related to the overall compression setting.

4. Keep the Preview option selected so you can see how your adjustments impact the quality of the resulting image.

5. Select your quality or dithering range and click OK. The Color Reduction Options dialog for GIF format does not offer a range.

CHAPTER FOUR

Working with Illustrator

I fondly remember my first chance to use Illustrator. Even in its initial version you could feel the fluid finesse of the Pen tool. The first couple of versions of Illustrator could easily be considered a PostScript editor with a graphic user interface, which was revolutionary nevertheless. But now in its twelfth version, Illustrator offers so many features and tools for creating and editing artwork, it's hard to recognize it from its simple beginnings.

Although Photoshop may get much of the attention, the truth is that Illustrator is the application that started Adobe. It's also the most mature application in the suite. With so many versions packed with features being released through the years, this powerhouse vector graphics tool is definitely a force to be reckoned with. Because it's such a deep, versatile tool, I can imagine that many people don't fully know its capabilities.

So with that in mind, I've come up with a set of tips and techniques for Illustrator that really runs the gamut of its capabilities and I hope enlightens you to some of Illustrator's lesser known but compelling features.

#31 Selecting Obscured Objects

Switching to Outline Mode

Many of us are so accustomed to working in Preview mode that we often forget Illustrator offers a simplified Outline mode (View > Outline) that's ideal for finding and selecting those hard to reach paths and points. Working in Outline mode can also be faster since Illustrator doesn't have to render all those fancy fills, strokes, and effects.

Have you ever found yourself working on a fairly complicated Illustrator document and spending more time trying to select the objects in your artwork than manipulating them? Selecting objects positioned on top of each other in Illustrator can be quite a challenge, if not downright annoying at times. The good news is that Illustrator offers a complete set of tools and commands devoted to helping you select just the objects you want.

Illustrator CS2 includes five tools for common selection tasks: Selection, Direct Selection, Group Selection, Magic Wand, and Lasso. All of these tools perform well in their own right, but they can seem rather limited when you attempt a more complex task such as selecting an object obscured by another. This is where the Next Object command comes in handy. To select an object below a selected object, choose Select > Next Object Below (**Figure 31a**). Notice that you can also choose Select > Next Object Above for the opposite situation. Keep in mind that these commands will skip over locked objects, as they rightfully should.

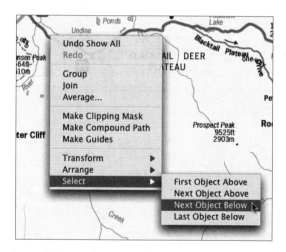

Figure 31a The Select > Next Object commands are available from the Object menu or via the contextual menu by Control-clicking (Mac) or right-clicking (Windows) on an object.

But if you're still having trouble selecting certain objects, head on over to the Layers palette. In its default setup, the Layers palette provides a row for every discrete object in your document. You can drill down to the very paths that make up an object and then click the Target icon ⊙ beside it to select it (**Figure 31b**).

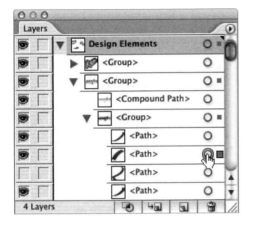

Figure 31b You can also use the Layers palette to access those hard to select objects or paths.

Selecting Same Attributes

The Magic Wand tool selects objects with attributes that are similar to the object you click with it. You can also select objects with similar attributes by selecting an object and choosing Select > Same > object attribute. From this submenu, a few additional attributes are available that aren't available via the Magic Wand tool. However, the Magic Wand tool offers tolerance settings, making it ideal for selecting attributes that may not be exactly the same.

#32 Isolating Selections with Lock and Hide

Isolating Groups within Groups

Illustrator CS2 introduces a handy way to navigate through a set of nested grouped objects. With the Selection tool, double-click a group. The group is selected and a thick-thin gray border appears around it. You can then move the objects within the isolated group selection, add objects into the current group level, or double-click nested groups to dive further into the group structure. Double-click anywhere outside the group to exit this isolated mode.

Two of the most useful tools for isolating selections are the Lock and Hide commands. Both commands have been available in a form much like their present form since the earliest incarnations of Illustrator. In fact, it would be tough to find an long-time Illustrator user who doesn't rely on these two commands just as much as the Pen tool. Their convenience is found in the sheer simplicity of what they accomplish.

The Lock command keeps objects visible but unselectable. To lock an object or set of objects, select the objects and then choose Object > Lock > Selection. (That's Command+2 (Mac) or Control+2 (Windows) for you keyboard-shortcut fans.) The Lock command is a great, on-the-fly method to quickly get objects out of your way, but an even more powerful option lurks just a little-known keyboard shortcut away: Select the object you want to focus on and press Shift+Option+Command+2 (Mac) or Shift+Alt+Control+2 (Windows). All other objects within your document are locked, in effect isolating your selection. This allows you to concentrate your efforts on the object selected. When you're ready to work with all the locked object again, choose Object > Unlock All.

The Hide command works in a similar fashion to Lock but instead makes the objects invisible and unselectable. To hide selected objects, choose Object > Hide > Selection. There's also a companion command to the above-mentioned locking command: Choose Shift+Option+Command-3 (Mac) or Shift+Alt+Control+3 (Windows) to hide all deselected artwork (**Figure 32**).

Figure 32 Attempting to edit a path within a complex document can be quite difficult. Using the secret Hide All Deselected command temporarily hides all artwork not selected, making it easy to edit the desired path.

#33 Creating Clipping Masks

If you've ever needed a fast way to crop or hide a portion of your artwork, you'll be happy to learn about clipping masks. A clipping mask is a special type of object whose shape masks out (or clips) artwork so that only the artwork within the confines of the mask are visible (**Figure 33**). Clipping masks can be made up of two or more objects. The masked objects can be vector or raster, but the mask itself must be a vector object.

Figure 33 Clipping masks make it effortless to use an object as a uniquely shaped frame for other objects. Here I've used the outside box as a clipping mask to clip the cylinder and bottom portion of the people.

To make a clipping mask, create the object you want to use as a mask. This is known as the clipping path. Remember that the clipping path must be vector based. Move the clipping path so it's above all the objects you want to mask in the stacking order. Use the Bring to Front command or the Layers palette to accomplish this. Next, select the clipping path and the objects you want to mask and then choose Object > Clipping Mask > Make. Feel free to commit the handy keyboard shortcut to memory: Command+7 (Mac) or Control+7 (Windows). Once the clipping mask is created, the clipping path is automatically assigned a fill and stroke value of None. This is something to be aware of if you decide to release the clipping mask back to a normal path (Object > Clipping Mask > Release) and wonder where your clipping path went. And although a clipping path reverts to no fill and stroke when made into a mask, that doesn't stop you from applying a new fill and stroke to it.

Clipping Mask for a Layer or Group

You can apply clipping masks on a layer or group level as well. Create your clipping path and then move it along with the objects you want to mask into a layer or group within the Layers palette. Next, bring the clipping path to the very top of the layer or group by dragging it up in the palette. Click on the layer or group name and then click the Make/Release Clipping Mask button at the bottom of the palette.

Selecting All Clipping Paths in a Document

If you're having trouble locating the clipping masks you've created in your document, you can quickly select them all by choosing Select > Object > Clipping Masks.

#34 Creating Compound Shapes

Illustrator's compound shapes feature makes it easy to create complex shapes made up of two or more basic shapes. Based on the original Pathfinder operations that have been around for some time now, compound shapes allow you to apply Pathfinder operations such as Add or Intersect to basic shapes to create a new shape while the underlying shapes remain editable.

Compound shapes are created via the Pathfinder palette (Window > Pathfinder). The four shape mode buttons, Add, Subtract, Intersect, and Exclude, result in compound shapes (**Figure 34a**). The best way to think of compound shapes is as live Pathfinder operations.

Figure 34a The top four buttons in the Pathfinder palette are the shape modes available for creating a compound shape.

To create a compound shape, create two or more basic shapes that overlap one another. To better illustrate the effect of a shape compound, fill the shapes with different colors. With the shapes selected, click the Add shape mode button in the Pathfinder palette. A compound shape is created, combining the basic shapes into one (**Figure 34b**). The object that was at the top of the stacking order determines the appearance of the other object in the compound shape. Switch to Outline mode (View > Outline). Notice that the original shapes still exist and remain editable (**Figure 34c**). You can switch back to Preview mode (View > Preview) and double-click the compound shape with the Selection tool to edit the underlying shapes.

Figure 34b You can achieve interesting results just by combining simple geometric shapes into a compound shape.

Copying Compound Shapes into Photoshop

You can copy compound shapes from Illustrator into Photoshop, where they end up as shape layers (see #24). Just make sure that if your compound shape has a stroke applied to it, that its weight is a whole number in points and doesn't use a round join. Otherwise, the compound shape will be rasterized, losing all its vector goodness.

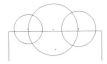

Figure 34c This artwork was created in a minute by using these four simple shapes and applying two shape modes: Add and Subtract. Switching to Outline mode reveals the actual shapes being used.

Try experimenting with all four shape modes. You can also create nested compound shapes by selecting a new shape and an existing compound shape and applying a shape mode again. To release a compound shape back to its basic set of shapes, select it and choose Release Compound Shape from the Pathfinder palette menu (**Figure 34d**).

Figure 34d When you want your artwork to revert to its basic shapes, select the Release Compound Shape command from the Pathfinder palette menu.

If you hold down the Option/Alt key when pressing a shape mode button, you can produce a combined single shape (a la the classic Pathfinder operations). Adobe refers to this type of shape as "fully expanded." The result is the same as applying a shape mode and then clicking the Expand button, which performs the Pathfinder operation and ultimately removes the dynamic, flexible nature that compound shapes offer.

#35 Working with Symbols

Symbols are objects that can be stored as source artwork and then be reused numerous times in a document as symbol instances. Edit or replace the symbol and all linked instances automatically update. Symbols make it easy to add a bit of random complexity to your artwork while saving you time and keeping file sizes to a minimum (**Figure 35a**).

Figure 35a Symbols make it incredibly easy for you to add multiple instances of your artwork by selecting a symbol from one of the sets available to you and literally spraying it onto the artboard.

A symbol can be made up of text, paths, embedded raster images, mesh objects and most groups of objects. You can even use Live Effects (see #36), brush strokes, and other symbol instances in a symbol. To create a symbol, select your artwork and click the New Symbol button in the Symbols palette (Window > Symbols). To be presented with the option to name the symbol, press the Option/Alt key when clicking New Symbol. You can hold down Shift if you'd like the selected artwork to automatically become an instance of the new symbol.

Once you've created your symbol, instances of it can be quickly added in volume using the Symbol Sprayer tool . With your symbol selected in the Symbols palette, choose the Symbol Sprayer tool in the Tools palette. Click and hold or click and drag to spray instances of your symbol onto the artboard, much like a paint spray can. Use the hidden symbolism tools under the Symbol Sprayer: Shifter, Scruncher, Sizer, Spinner, Stainer, Screener, and Styler to

Keys to Working with Symbolism Tools

You should be aware of a few special keys when working with the symbolism tools. You can adjust the spraying radius using the bracket keys on the keyboard: "[" for a smaller radius and "]" for a larger one. To delete instances, hold down the Option/Alt key while spraying. Last but not least, double-click the Symbol Sprayer tool to display the Symbolism Tools Options dialog. Within this dialog, click through the various tools to learn the specific modifier keys each tool uses to control its effect.

interactively tweak your instances and make them appear more natural and distinct from one another (**Figure 35b**).

Figure 35b Use the various symbolism tools hidden under the Symbol Sprayer tool to make your artwork appear more random and diverse in size, rotation, color, and so on.

To redefine your symbol and automatically update all the linked instances, drag an instance of your symbol from the Symbols palette to the artboard. With the instance selected, click the Break Link to Symbol button ▨ in the Symbols palette. Make your edits to the artwork and then drag it back on top of the original symbol in the Symbols palette while holding down the Option/Alt key (you can only do this if you're using entirely new artwork). This replaces the old symbol with the new and all its instances are dynamically updated.

#36 Using Live Effects

If you compare the Filter and Effect menus in Illustrator, you'll notice that they offer similar options (**Figure 36a**). Both set of commands mostly change the appearance of your artwork. The key difference is where effects remain "live" or editable, allowing you to adjust the underlying artwork and the effect settings. Filters are applied permanently to your artwork and can't be changed, much like Photoshop filters. Effects can even be applied to bitmap objects you've embedded in your document. Although effects provide an incredible level of flexibility, filters are useful when you need to directly edit the resulting artwork produced.

Adjusting Raster Effects Settings

Since raster effects are pixel based, it's important to check that the raster effect settings match your output quality settings before applying them. Choose Effect > Document Raster Effects Settings to see the current settings and adjust them if necessary. If your artwork is destined for any output higher in resolution than an inkjet printer, consider adjusting the Resolution option to High (300 ppi).

Figure 36a Although the Filter and Effect menus share many similar options, the Effect menu is the best choice for ultimate flexibility since the effects continue to be editable.

Once you've applied an effect, you can revisit and edit its settings at any time by double-clicking the effect name in the Appearance palette (see #37). You can apply multiple effects to an object, and they'll appear stacked in the Appearance palette. Here you can easily reorder or remove them (**Figure 36b**).

Working with Illustrator

Figure 36b Once an effect is applied, you can double-click it within the Appearance palette to adjust its settings. You can also have multiple effects on any given item.

Many of the effects under the Illustrator Effect menu reshape your underlying artwork while keeping it vector-based. Some of the more compelling effects in this group are 3D, Convert to Shape, and Distort & Transform. They can radically change the appearance of your artwork, but can make it difficult to edit the underlying artwork. When this happens, switch to Outline mode (View > Outline), which hides the effects and exposes the source artwork, making it easier to edit.

The other effects are considered raster effects, which blend pixels with your vector-based artwork. The majority of the effects located in the Photoshop Effect menu are raster effects and are only available in RGB mode. You can switch your document to RGB by choosing File > Document Color Mode > RGB Mode, but be sure this is acceptable in your color workflow.

#37 Exploring the Appearance Palette

Saving Graphic Styles

Once you've decided on a set of attributes you would like to apply to other objects, you can save it as a reusable graphic style (see #74). Simply drag the object with the applied attributes into the Graphic Styles palette (Window > Graphic Styles). To apply the graphic style to new objects, select the object and click your graphic style.

The Appearance palette may seem like a sophisticated Info palette at first glance, simply reporting the appearance attributes of the selected object. But looking deeper, you'll see that this palette allows you to directly interact with these characteristics, build upon them, and then save them as a graphic style to apply to other objects

This means that just about any object can be made up of multiple fills, strokes, and live effects. To top it off, any of these fills, strokes, or effects (see #36) can include discrete transparency settings, or you can apply a global setting to the entire object or layer. The Appearance palette is designed to manage it all (**Figure 37a**).

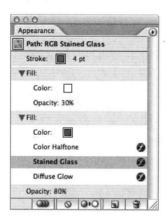

Figure 37a The Appearance palette is your command center for controlling every minute detail of an object's overall appearance. Objects can have multiple fills, strokes, blending modes, and effects applied to them.

To add multiple attributes to an object, such as multiple strokes, select the attribute in the Appearance palette and click the Duplicate Selected Item button. With the duplicated attribute selected, you can apply a different attribute characteristic, for example, stroke weight, color, opacity, blending mode, or live effect. You can reorder attributes by dragging them within the palette just like you drag layers in the Layers palette. Keep in mind that you can have multiple effects on an object or certain items, such as individual fills or strokes (**Figure 37b**). Ordering effects and other items can dramatically change the overall appearance of an object. To delete a selected attribute, click the Delete Selected Item button. When you select an object that contains other objects, such as a layer, group, or text object, a Contents row appears in the palette. Double-click the Contents row to drill into the object's contents. As you start working with the Appearance palette, you'll soon realize just how powerful and flexible it truly is.

Figure 37b Applying multiple fills, strokes, effects, and so on, you can create some truly compelling results. All of the objects shown are basic circles with various style attributes applied to them.

#**38** Distorting Artwork with Envelopes

An envelope distorts selected objects to conform to its outer shape. Envelopes make it simple to bend and warp artwork or design custom-styled type. Almost any shape can be defined as an envelope and then edited using the normal path and type tools. You can also use any of the preset warp shapes or a mesh grid as an envelope.

To distort artwork using your own envelope shape, create the objects you want to distort and then the object you want to use as the envelope. Make sure your envelope shape is at the top of the stacking order by selecting it and choosing Object > Arrange > Bring to Front or rearranging it in the Layers palette. Then select the target objects and the envelope shape, and choose Object > Envelope Distort > Make with Top Object (**Figure 38a**). The underlying artwork automatically assumes the shape of the envelope, although you can also manually edit the envelope path at any time.

Figure 38a A simple shape can be used as an envelope to distort just about any other artwork.

If you'd rather use a preset warp shape to distort your selected artwork, choose Object > Envelope Distort > Make with Warp. The Warp Options dialog pops up with several preset warp styles and options to select from (**Figure 38b**). Bear in mind that these are merely preset warp shapes; once applied you're still able to edit the envelope shape.

Working with Illustrator

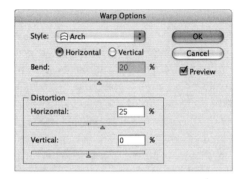

Figure 38b The Warp Options dialog includes
various preset warps to choose from and then
adjust further.

You also have the option of using a rectangular grid, known as a
mesh grid, to distort your artwork (**Figure 38c**). With your objects
selected, choose Object > Envelope Distort > Make with Mesh. Decide
on the number of rows and columns you want to use in the Envelope
Mesh dialog and click OK. With the envelope mesh applied, you can
use the Direct Selection tool to manipulate the mesh intersections
or use the Mesh tool to add more intersections.

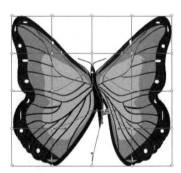

Figure 38c You can use a mesh grid
as a basis of your envelope transform
and then distort your artwork by
editing the intersections of the grid.

#38: Distorting Artwork with Envelopes

#39 Using Live Trace

Years ago, Adobe Streamline was the definitive tool to take your scanned bitmap images and convert them into vector artwork so you could continue to work on them within Illustrator. Now this can be done directly within Illustrator CS2 using the new Live Trace feature. Live Trace automatically converts your placed images into vector graphics with a click of a button. If you're not satisfied with the default results, change the settings (or the placed image) and Illustrator dynamically updates the vector artwork in response.

Although there are a couple of different ways to apply a Live Trace to your selected image, the most convenient is to use the new Control palette (see #17). Once you click the Live Trace button (**Figure 39a**) in the Control palette, your image is immediately converted to vector artwork.

Applying Live Trace and Live Paint Together

If you grow tired of using the Control palette and having to click the Live Trace and then the Live Paint button to access Live Paint, try the two-in-one menu command. With your bitmap image selected, choose Object > Live Trace > Make and Convert to Live Paint. Illustrator then applies a Live Trace to your image using your current settings and then converts the tracing to a Live Paint group in one fell swoop.

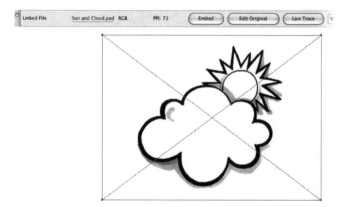

Figure 39a When you have an image selected in Illustrator, the new Control palette offers up a big, simple button to apply a Live Trace to the image.

Notice that once you apply Live Trace, the Control palette options change, presenting new options for your tracing. You can select a different tracing preset, adjust the threshold and minimum area, select different preview options, expand the artwork into editable paths, or convert the tracing to a Live Paint group (**Figure 39b**). All of these options except Expand and Live Paint allow you to freely experiment with different settings and automatically update the tracing. After you decide on a set of tracing settings you're pleased with, convert your tracing to a Live Paint group (see #40) by clicking the Live Paint button.

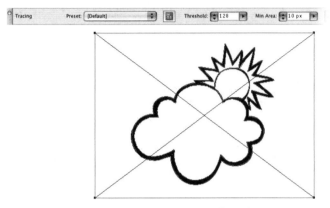

Figure 39b After you've applied a Live Trace, the Control palette presents appropriate options to adjust the Live Trace settings or convert the tracing to paths or a Live Paint group.

#**40** Using Live Paint

Detecting Gaps

When working with a tracing in a Live Paint group, there may be times when you have small gaps in your artwork that you'd like to treat as edges. As if Live Paint wasn't powerful enough, it can even detect gaps in your artwork and automatically fill them. With your Live Paint group selected, choose Object > Live Paint > Gap Options. Enable the Gap Detection option and adjust any other settings. To show the detected gaps while not in this dialog, choose View > Show Live Paint Gaps.

The new Live Paint feature in Illustrator CS2 lets you paint directly in the areas between strokes as you would color a coloring book. You no longer need to concern yourself with the underlying objects and stacking order that result in the artwork. Live Paint automatically detects the gaps, boundaries, and areas throughout your artwork and makes them available as edges and faces you can quickly and easily paint. Even though you can apply Live Paint to any conventional vector artwork, it's a perfect complement to the new Live Trace feature (see #39).

To start using the Live Paint feature, you must first convert your selection into a special type of group called a Live Paint group. To create a Live Paint group from a Live Trace, select the tracing and click the Live Paint button in the Control palette. To make a Live Paint group from selected vector artwork, choose the Live Paint Bucket tool from the Tools palette and click the artwork (**Figure 40a**). Note that some types of objects—type, brushes, and bitmap images—can't be converted into a Live Paint group. To get around this you can convert type to outlines, expand brushes, and use Live Trace images.

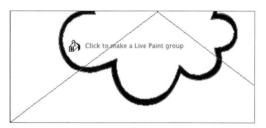

Figure 40a To convert artwork into a Live Paint group, simply click it with the Live Paint Bucket tool.

Once your artwork has been converted to a Live Paint group, you can continue to use the Live Paint Bucket tool to pick colors, swatches, or styles and paint them into faces or edges of the Live

Paint group. Hold down the Option/Alt key to temporarily switch to the Eyedropper tool to sample an appearance from another object. The Live Paint Bucket tool nicely highlights the available faces and edges as you hover over them (**Figure 40b**).

Figure 40b As soon as artwork is converted to a Live Paint group you can start painting it in a natural manner as you would a coloring book. It's actually kind of fun. Areas are highlighted to show you what will be filled.

You also can select multiple faces and edges at once using the Live Paint Selection tool 🔧. Use this tool when you want to select multiple portions of your Live Paint group first and then apply a fill or stroke.

If you create a Live Paint group from artwork that didn't originate from a Live Trace, an interesting effect reveals itself when you move the underlying objects that make up the group. Double-click your Live Paint group with the Selection tool to isolate the group. Then move one of the objects and watch as the color of the Live Paint faces automatically follows along—hence the "live" in Live Paint (**Figure 40c**).

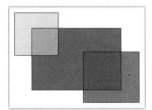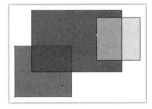

Figure 40c Live Paint groups are just that…live. Move the underlying objects around and the painted faces follow.

CHAPTER FIVE

Working with InDesign

Among the main applications that make up the Creative Suite, InDesign could be considered the new kid on the block, with its initial version released in 1999. But that doesn't equate to it being any less feature-rich or powerful than the 18-year-old applications in the suite. InDesign was born out of a need to create a modern page layout application that could lead the industry and handle today's demands for multiple types of output. Regardless if the final destination is print, an Acrobat file, a Web site, or a combination of these formats, InDesign is up to the task.

With the release of InDesign CS2, Adobe has taken an already versatile page layout tool and made it even more convenient and flexible to work with. New features such as Object Styles and Anchored Objects let you focus on designing and laying out your pages instead of hunting down inconsistencies and stray page elements.

It's evident with this fourth major release of InDesign that Adobe has no plans on easing up on the amount of features and tools packed into each release. So with this in mind, I've assembled a set of techniques that attempts to cover the most ground throughout this truly remarkable page layout application.

#41 Working with Master Pages

Master pages have been around for nearly as long as desktop publishing, but many users may not realize how helpful they can be when producing a long document. Master pages allow you to define how elements such as text, graphics, and guides will appear on any pages based on the master. The beauty of this approach is that you can return to the master and reposition or change any of those elements, and those changes will be reflected across the entire document.

You can create a master page from scratch or use a page you already started laying out in the document. To create a new blank master, open the Pages palette and choose New Master from the palette menu. Alternatively, press Command (Mac) or Control (Windows) while clicking the New Page button at the bottom of the palette. To create a master based on an existing page or spread in your document, select it and choose Save as Master from the palette menu. I prefer the more straightforward method of dragging the page or spread to the Master area in the palette (**Figure 41a**). This works just as well.

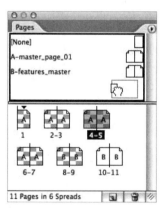

Figure 41a You can simply drag a page or spread into the Master area to make a master page from it.

What makes master pages in InDesign even more effective is that they can be based on existing master pages. This allows you to set up a parent master page and create several different child masters from it. Say, for example, that you have a header bar that you want on all pages, but on certain pages you want a sidebar along with the header bar. You can easily accomplish this by basing the sidebar master on the header bar master. To base a master on another master, drag the master you want to use as a basis (the parent master) on top of another master (the child master) (**Figure 41b**).

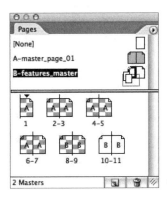

Figure 41b Drag and drop a parent master page on top of another master to create a parent-child relationship.

When you want to apply a master page to a document page, drag the master on top of the page icon in the Pages palette. To apply a master to a page spread, drag the master to a corner of the spread until a black outline surrounds the entire spread and then release it (**Figure 41c**). If you want to apply a master to multiple pages at once, select them in the Pages palette and hold down Option/Alt as you click the master you want to apply.

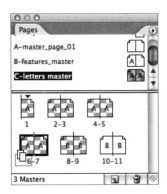

Figure 41c To apply a master to a page, drag it on top of the page. To apply a master to a spread, drag it over the page's corners until the entire spread has a thick black outline around it.

(continued on next page)

Auto Page Numbering

Another timesaving advantage of using master pages is the ability to set up automatic page numbering. Create a text frame on your master page where you would like the page number to appear. Click into the frame with the Type tool and then choose Type > Insert Special Character > Auto Page Number. A letter is inserted that corresponds to the prefix letter of your master. You can then select this special character and style it just as you would any other text.

#41: Working with Master Pages

Sometimes you may want to change the contents or layout of a master page. Simply double-click its page icon in the Pages palette to go to it within the document and make your changes. Any pages based on the master will automatically update. If you need to make changes to master page objects on a specific page, you can override them. Press Command+Shift (Mac) or Control+Shift (Windows) as you click the master page object. This will release it from the master, allowing you to edit its attributes while keeping an association to it. Once you override a master object attribute, that attribute will not update if it is later changed on the master. However, attributes that haven't been overridden will update. For example, you can change the fill and size of an object by overriding those attributes on a certain page, but when the master object's position changes, the overridden object will change position as well. This level of control is what makes master pages so powerful.

#42 Fitting Contents within Frames

When you place or paste graphics within existing frames, they rarely conform to one another. You can go through the trouble of manually resizing the graphic or frame so the two fit together, but why bother? InDesign includes a set of commands and corresponding Control bar buttons to help achieve a perfect fit every time (**Figure 42**).

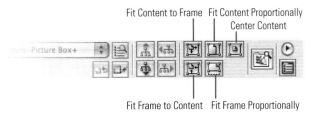

Fit Content to Frame   Fit Content Proportionally
Center Content

Fit Frame to Content   Fit Frame Proportionally

Figure 42 The content fitting buttons found on the Control palette make quick work of fitting graphics to frames and vice versa.

To fit content to its frame, select the frame and either click the appropriate Control palette button or choose Object > Fitting and one of the options that follow:

Fit Content to Frame: Resizes the content so it fits the frame, even if it means changing the proportions. The content will appear stretched if it's a different proportion than the frame, so this command is only useful in rare occasions in which you don't mind that the contents are distorted.

Fit Frame to Content: Changes the frame's dimensions to match the content. Use this option if the content can't be resized, and you want the frame to conform to the content's proportions.

(continued on next page)

Crop with a Dynamic Preview

Although the content fitting options are incredibly useful, there are times when you'll want to manually crop content to its frame. InDesign even makes this painless by offering a dynamic preview while cropping. With the Direct Selection or Position tool selected, click and hold on the frame's content. Anything outside of the frame will be ghosted back. Then drag the content to the desired position within the frame. You can also click and hold on the frame handles to crop with a dynamic preview in this manner.

Fit Content Proportionally: Resizes the content proportionally to fit the frame's proportions. This ensures that the content will not get cropped, but you can end up with empty space if the two do not share the same proportions. This is probably one of the most useful options of the bunch. Try using this option and then follow it with the Fit Frame to Content option if you want the frame dimension to loosely define the working proportions but the content to ultimately decide them.

Fill Frame Proportionally: Resizes the content proportionally to fill the frame. This option will most likely result in your content being cropped unless its proportions are the same as the frame.

Center Content: Doesn't resize anything but instead ensures that the content is perfectly centered both horizontally and vertically within the frame.

#43 Using the Story Editor

The Story Editor got its start in PageMaker, where users quickly appreciated its usefulness. It allows you to focus on editing text in a word-processor-like view without being distracted by formatting and layout. InDesign's Story Editor improves upon the one in PageMaker, making it feel more like a word processor. You can view hidden characters, perform find/change actions, and check spelling (**Figure 43a**).

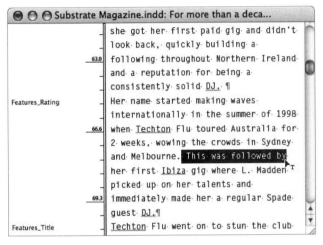

Figure 43a The Story Editor window allows you to focus on the text in your document without being distracted by the layout.

To open a story in Story Editor, click an insertion point in a frame or select a text frame (or several of them) and choose Edit > Edit in Story Editor. To switch back to Layout, choose Edit > Edit in Layout or close the window. You can toggle between these views by using the easy to remember keyboard shortcut: Command+Y (Mac) or Control+Y (Windows).

Once you're in a Story Editor window, you can concentrate on adding new text or editing existing text. But don't mistake the simplicity of this view as being limited. There are plenty of tasks you can do without leaving the Story Editor.

(continued on next page)

Open Multiple Instances of a Story Editor

Save yourself some time in those intense text-editing sessions when you're jumping back and forth between locations in a long story. You can open multiple instances of the same window and scroll to different locations in them. To create a new instance of a window, make sure the Story Editor window is active, and then choose Window > Arrange > New Window. This technique is useful for similar situations in Layout mode.

Story Editor Preferences

Be sure to check out the Story Editor Display preferences available in InDesign's Preferences dialog. From there you can decide on font, colors (both text and background), cursor, and anti-aliasing options used in the Story Editor.

Here are some of the possible functions you can perform in a Story Editor window:

- **View and apply style sheets:** Any styles applied appear in the left style name column. Apply paragraph and character styles as you would in Layout mode.

- **Check spelling:** You can check spelling in the story as you would in Layout mode. Turn on dynamic spelling (Edit > Spelling > Dynamic Spelling) to have InDesign check spelling as you type. Red squiggly underlines indicate misspellings as in Microsoft Word.

- **Drag and drop text:** InDesign CS2 now supports drag-and-drop text. Select your text and then hover over the selection until the new drag-drop text cursor appears ▶_T . Drag the selection to a new location and drop it.

- **View and edit overset text:** Text not visible in its frame is known as overset text. A red line runs alongside any overset text that occurs in your story. The Story Editor makes it possible to see and edit the overset text unlike in Layout mode where you need to expand the text frame before editing.

- **View and edit a story in its entirety:** Possibly the least obvious feature of the Story Editor is that it allows you to view a story in one complete window regardless of whether the story text is on multiple pages in the document layout.

#44 Defining Nested Styles

Nested styles are one of the innovative ways InDesign saves you trips to the Character Styles palette. Within a paragraph style, you can set up character styles to apply to a range of text based on a certain length or character and then automatically switch to another nested character style or revert to the base paragraph style. For example, you could define a character style to run through to the first sentence or after the first colon. This makes nested styles ideal for creating run-in headings that are popular in magazines (**Figure 44a**). But this is just one obvious application for them.

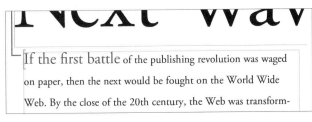

Figure 44a Nested styles are perfect for handling run-in headings where the first few words or the first sentence is styled differently than the rest of the paragraph.

Before defining nested styles, create the paragraph and subsequent character styles you want to use. Double-click on the paragraph style in the Paragraph Styles palette. Next, click Drop Caps and Nested Styles on the menu list on the left of the dialog. Click the New Nested Style button and choose one of your character styles from the first menu labeled [None]. Then decide which item will determine the end of the character style formatting. You can enter a character or number, or select a special option from the menu (**Figure 44b**). Although you can type a whole word in the field, only the first character will be used. You can click on "through" to switch it to "up to," which changes the character style range from including the ending character to not doing so. Then add as many other nested styles as you want and order them using the up and down buttons.

(continued on next page)

End Nested Style Character

Nested styles allow you to use most any character, word, or sentence length to determine when they end, but if you can't decide on anything in particular, try using the End Nested Style character. This special invisible character explicitly ends a nested style for you. Choose End Nested Style Character from the far right menu of your nested style row. Then once you apply your paragraph style with the nested style within it, choose Type > Insert Special Character > End Nested Style Here, to stop your nested style.

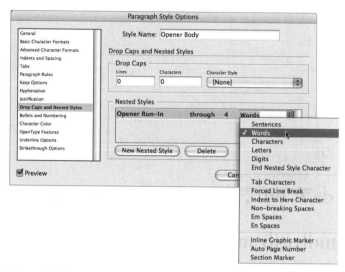

Figure 44b You can enter a character or choose from the menu that includes special characters or other factors to end your nested style.

Once you've defined your nested styles within the paragraph style, all paragraphs that previously had the style applied automatically update. It's even more fun to watch the nested styles switch as you type. Create a new text frame by dragging a rectangle with the Type tool. Then select the paragraph style with the nested styles and start typing. Watch as the formatting automatically switches as you trigger the determining characters or factors.

#45 Repeating Transformations

Illustrator allows you to repeat your last transformation and has for quite some time. When you move, scale, or rotate an object and then select Object > Transform Again, Illustrator automatically performs the transformation again on your selection. InDesign CS2 carries over this indispensable command and supercharges it. InDesign CS2 not only makes it possible to repeat the last transformation, but it remembers all the transformations you recently applied to an object and allows you to repeat the transformation sequence to other objects.

To access the four repeat transformation options choose Object > Transform Again (**Figure 45a**). But make sure you've actually transformed an object first by moving, scaling, shearing, or rotating it. Then select the object or objects you want to apply the transformations to and choose a Transform Again option.

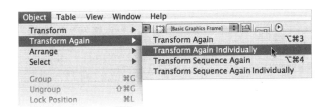

Figure 45a The Transform Again options are located in the Object menu. Notice that some of the commands offer keyboard shortcuts.

It's a little difficult to understand the difference between the Transform Again options at first. Here's a description of each and what to consider when deciding between them:

- **Transform Again:** Applies only the most recent transformation to a selection. This is probably the option you'll use most often for typical situations, so you might want to memorize its keyboard shortcut: Option+Command+3 (Mac) or Alt+Control+3 (Windows).

(continued on next page)

- **Transform Again Individually:** Works just like Transform Again, but when you have multiple objects selected, it applies the previously applied transformation on each object individually instead of treating the objects as a group. This is helpful since each object is transformed on its own axis, saving you from having to separately transform them (**Figure 45b**).

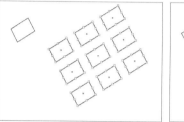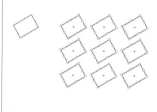

Figure 45b Here's the difference between Transform Again (left) and Transform Again Individually (right). Transform Again rotates the entire selection, whereas Transform Again Individually rotates each object.

- **Transform Sequence Again:** Applies the most recent sequence of transformations to a selection. Because InDesign remembers all the transformations applied to an object until you transform another object, it lets you move, scale, skew, and rotate an object, and then performs all those transformations to a selection of objects all at once.

- **Transform Sequence Again Individually:** Applies the last-used sequence of transformations to your selection to each selected object independently. Just like Transform Again Individually, this option respects each object's axis within the selection and transforms them simultaneously.

#46 Applying Effects

One feature that defines InDesign as a truly modern page layout tool is its built-in ability to apply raster-based effects and have other objects interact with them. There's no need to enlist Photoshop or a third-party plug-in to apply a drop shadow or feather the edges of an object. You can even apply transparency effects to an object as you would in Photoshop and Illustrator.

Before applying an effect, it's a good idea to temporarily increase your display preview to high quality (View > Display Performance > High Quality Display) so that you have a truer preview of the effect.

To apply a drop shadow to a selected object, choose Object > Drop Shadow (**Figure 46a**). Select the Drop Shadow and Preview check boxes. You can then adjust the blend mode, opacity, offset, blur, spread, and noise to your liking. Choose a color from your list of swatches or select a different option from the Color menu to use a new color.

Spread and Noise Options

New to InDesign CS2 are the Spread and Noise options found in the Drop Shadow and Feather dialogs. The Spread option controls the area of the blur in a drop shadow, whereas the Noise option adds random artifacts to generate a rough grain in the effect. Adding noise to an effect helps it to interact more seamlessly with background objects and tends to result in less banding when printed.

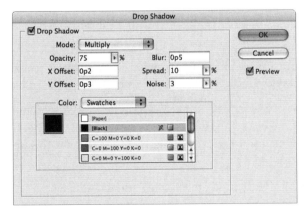

Figure 46a The Drop Shadow dialog provides many of the options you're used to seeing in Photoshop.

(continued on next page)

The feather effect softens the edges of an object by fading them to transparent. To feather a selected object, choose Object > Feather (**Figure 46b**). Select the Feather and Preview check boxes and set feather width. This is the distance over which the feather fades from opaque to transparent. Then choose a corner option and optionally add noise.

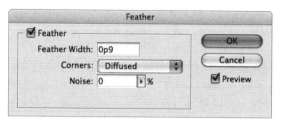

Figure 46b The Feather dialog makes it easy to apply a feather effect onto images or other artwork without having to leave InDesign.

Here are a few other points to keep in mind when working with effects:

- Effects can be applied to any object whether it was created in InDesign or placed into InDesign from another application.

- Drop shadows and feathers are applied to the contents of a frame including text, if the frame has a fill of none. Give the frame a fill color, and the frame will receive the effect instead.

- These effects are flattened when printed. Although InDesign does its best to maintain the appearance you've created, it's worthwhile to use the Flattener Preview palette (Window > Output > Flattener Preview) to see which objects are affected.

- Effects are live so you can adjust an applied effect on a selected object at any time by choosing the effect again from the Object menu.

#47 Anchoring Objects

InDesign has always made it intuitive and easy to work with inline graphics. Paste an object into a text frame and it behaves like any other character or word in the block of text, flowing along with the text. The only catch was that the object had to remain inside the text. Well, that is until now. InDesign CS2 introduces the ability to anchor objects to text where the object can now overlap or exist outside the text frame. This feature is a real boon to anyone who's ever struggled to keep sidebars associated with the main story as it flowed (take this book for instance).

You create anchored objects as you would an inline graphic in previous versions of InDesign: Select the object you want to anchor and cut it. Click an insertion point within the target text frame by using the Type tool or by double-clicking the text frame with the Selection tool. Then simply paste the object. The object is anchored to the text using the default positioning of Inline (inline positioned anchored objects used to be called inline graphics).

Once you've anchored the object to text, you can change its position type so you can move the object to any location on the page. Use the Selection tool to select the newly created anchored object and choose Object > Anchored Object > Options. From this dialog (**Figure 47a**), change the Position menu to Custom and click OK.

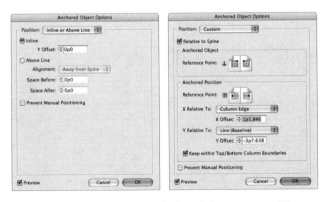

Figure 47a The Anchored Objects Options dialog presents a different set of options depending on which Position menu option you've selected.

(continued on next page)

#47: Anchoring Objects

Relative to Spine

As if anchored objects weren't ridiculously helpful in their own right, they also include the option to automatically adjust their position relative to a spread's spine. This means that if you move the anchored text frame or it reflows to the opposite side of a spread, the anchored object automatically repositions itself accordingly – for example, to the right of the text frame instead of left. To enable this feature, bring up the Anchored Objects Options and select Relative to Spine. Then decide on a reference point by clicking on one of the eight squares on either page icon.

Two new text alignment options—Away From Spine and Towards Spine—provide similar functionality for text. Look for them next to the standard alignment options in the Control palette and paragraph styles.

A little blue anchor icon ⚓ indicates that the object is a custom positioned anchored object. You can then use the Selection tool to reposition your anchored object anywhere on the page and have its position remain relative to the anchored text (**Figure 47b**). Is it just me, or did page layout seem to just get a whole lot easier?

Figure 47b As the frame of the anchored text is repositioned or reflows, the anchored object moves along with it.

#48 Using Object Styles

Object styles in InDesign CS2 do for objects what paragraph and character styles do for text. With one click you can consistently apply the same graphical treatment to a series of objects. Then, if you change your mind about a stroke width, color, or effect, update the object style and all the objects with styles applied automatically update.

The most straightforward way to define an object style is to base it on an object you've already created and styled. Open the Object Styles palette (Window > Object Styles). With the object selected, hold down the Option/Alt key as you click the Create New Style button at the bottom of the palette. Holding down Option/Alt displays the Object Style Options dialog (**Figure 48**), giving you an opportunity to name the style and adjust any of the options before the style is created. Select any of the categories and adjust their options as needed. Categories not checked will not be applied to the style. This behavior is similar to character styles where an object's original attributes will not be overridden or cleared unless specified by the style.

Redefining Object Styles

To redefine a style based on an object whose attributes you've overridden, choose Redefine Object Style from the Object Styles palette menu. The style definition instantly updates with your overrides, and all objects based on the style follow suit. I find this method more convenient and interactive for editing a style rather than digging through a style's options dialog.

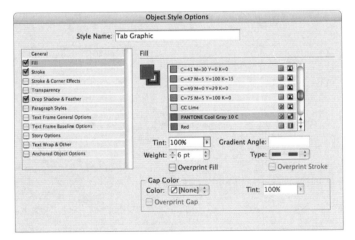

Figure 48 The Object Style Options dialog includes a plethora of options that you can assign to a style.

(continued on next page)

See What's Enabled and Overridden

You can instantly see which categories are enabled on an object style without opening the Object Style Options dialog. Hover over the style name with your cursor and a tool tip pops up detailing the categories the object style enables. If the selected object has overrides, the tool tip informs you of this and indicates what's been overridden.

Once you've defined an object style, you can easily apply it to other selected objects, groups, or frames by selecting it in the Object Styles palette or Control palette. Object styles also appear in the Quick Apply list (see #49). And as with other styles, you can double-click the name of the object style to edit its options and then have your changes automatically reflected on any objects that have the style applied.

#49 Applying Styles Quickly

As you begin to take advantage of using styles throughout your documents, you may find that applying styles can become unwieldy when you have several to choose from. InDesign CS2 offers two new timesaving features, Quick Apply and the Next Style option, to quickly find and apply styles, no matter how many styles you are working with.

Quick Apply lets you promptly locate a style and apply it by typing part of its name. Your fingers never have to leave the keyboard. Quick Apply finds paragraph and character styles and also includes object styles (see #48) when an object is selected. To use Quick Apply, select the text or object you want to apply a style to and press Command+Return (Mac) or Control+Enter (Windows) to bring up the Quick Apply list (**Figure 49a**). Begin typing part of the style name and the list narrows the search results the more you type. You don't have to type the name exactly; any part of the style name will work. You can use the up and down arrow keys on your keyboard to change the selection highlight in the results. Once the style you want is highlighted in the list, press Return or Enter to apply it. Press Shift+Return/Enter to apply the style and leave the Quick Apply list open. This is handy for when you want to apply both a paragraph and character style to a selection in record time.

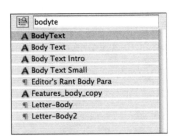

Figure 49a The Quick Apply list lets you type parts of a style name to select it and then quickly apply it.

Suppose you have a run of text that consists of a headline, subhead, and body text. Normally, you'd have to click into each one to apply individual paragraph styles. InDesign CS2 lets you define a Next Style setting in a paragraph style so that you can apply a succession of styles to multiple paragraphs at once. To do this,

(continued on next page)

---

edit a style by double-clicking on it and choose another paragraph style from the Next Style menu in the General category options (**Figure 49b**).

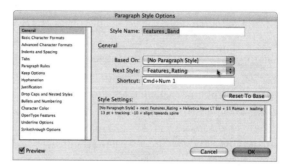

Figure 49b Selecting a style from the Next Style menu automates the switching of paragraph styles while you're typing or makes it possible to apply sequential styles at once.

After you've established all your next styles in your paragraph styles, you can see them in action. As soon as you start a new paragraph from this style, InDesign automatically assigns the defined next style to it. You can apply paragraph styles with next styles assigned to a selection of paragraphs at once by Control-clicking (Mac) or right-clicking (Windows) on the style name and choosing Apply {*style name*} then Next Style from the contextual menu (**Figure 49c**). As long as there are next styles defined, the next paragraph style will be applied.

Figure 49c After you've selected multiple paragraphs, open this contextual menu on a style with a next style applied to it to instantly apply multiple styles at once.

#**50** Working with Books

Books are a collection of InDesign documents that can share styles and colors between them. Breaking up a long document into shorter ones managed through a book offers many benefits. It keeps the file sizes to a minimum, and if for some horrible reason a document becomes corrupt, you potentially lose only a handful of pages instead of your entire document. Using books also makes sense if you're working within a team, allowing you to divvy up the work across documents. Be sure to take advantage of Version Cue in situations like these so you and your team members don't accidentally overwrite each other's work. You can also use books to collect documents of different page orientations or sizes into one set.

Here's how to create a book from individual documents and start working with it:

1. Choose File > New > Book and then decide on a location and name for your book file. The saved book shows up as a palette in InDesign but behaves like a document. If you close it, you must choose File > Open to reopen it.

2. Add your documents to the book by dragging them into the Book palette from the Finder (Mac) or File Explorer (Windows). You can also click the Add Documents button ⊕ on the Book palette.

3. Rearrange your documents in the Book palette by dragging them up or down as you would layers in the Layers palette. The order of the documents determines the page number sequence (**Figure 50a**).

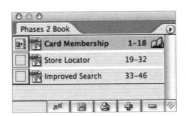

Figure 50a The Book palette shows all the associated documents and their page numbers. Rearrange the documents to change their order in the book and page numbering.

(continued on next page)

(continued on next page)

Converting Documents to Books

If your document is fast approaching 20 pages, you may want to consider breaking it up and organizing it as a book. You first need to have manageable pieces to work with. Decide on ideal break points throughout the document such as sections, chapters, or its page signature setup (usually 8, 16, or 32 pages). Then make a number of copies of the document and selectively delete the other pages in each copy based on these break points. For example, in the first copy, delete all except Chapter One, in the second copy, delete all but Chapter Two, and so on.

Synchronizing Styles Across Books

By default the first document in a book is designated as the style source. This means that the document will be used to synchronize the styles and swatches throughout the book. You can choose another document as the source by clicking the empty box to the left of its name in the Book palette. The style source icon 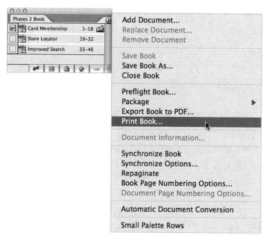 will then switch to this document. Click the Synchronize button to sync your styles and swatches across all the documents in the book.

4. Save the changes to your book by clicking the Save Book button on the Book palette.

5. Open documents within the book by double-clicking their name in the Book palette. You should always open booked documents through the Book palette, especially when working collaboratively. This ensures that the documents remain synchronized with the book and its pagination.

6. Print or output an entire book or just certain documents within it. If you want to print or output the entire book, be sure none of the documents are selected by clicking in the gray area below the document names. If you want to print or output certain documents in the book, you first need to select them. Then with either no documents selected or certain ones selected, go to the Book palette menu and choose one of the options listed: Preflight, Package for GoLive or Print, Export to PDF, or Print (**Figure 50b**).

Figure 50b You can print or output a book just as you would a document. The Book palette menu lists all the options available to you.

CHAPTER SIX

Working with GoLive

I'm not ashamed to admit that I built many of my first Web sites back in the '90s using an earlier version of GoLive. Even then the application took the concept of page layout and successfully brought it over to visual Web page design. If you're new to Web design or just new to GoLive, you'll appreciate GoLive's approach to designing Web pages.

Given its ease of use and Adobe's trademark user interface, GoLive is likely the favorite Web page design application of most designers. One of the main aspects that makes GoLive so easy to learn and start working with is that it acts and behaves more like a page layout application and less like a Web coding tool. This isn't to say you can't use it to hand code if you're so inclined, but GoLive really shines when you're laying out a Web page like you would a page in InDesign.

With this latest release of GoLive, Adobe has added innovative features for visually designing Web pages with Cascading Stylesheets (CSS). It boasts tighter integration with the other applications in the suite and tools for designing pages for mobile devices. GoLive CS2 is packaged with the Premium version of the Creative Suite, making it available to a new set of Adobe users who might have once shied away from Web site design. So let's look at what this distinctive Web page design application can now do.

#51 Exploring the Tools

In earlier versions of GoLive, what looked like a toolbox was really just the Objects palette, which allowed you to drag precoded objects onto your page. GoLive CS2 introduces a much welcomed, dedicated Tools palette (**Figure 51**).

Figure 51 The introduction of true tools (including Adobe standard tools) to the new Tools palette in GoLive CS2 is a welcome addition.

The Objects palette is now grouped with the tools but you can separate them if you'd like (see #5). Let's explore these new tools and see just how they're used.

Standard Editing tool: Perform common tasks such as moving and resizing objects and editing text. This is essentially the tool that was implied in earlier versions of GoLive.

Object Selection tool: Select and move any object except text, much like the Selection tool found in Illustrator and InDesign. Double-click a layer with this tool to switch to the Standard Editing tool and edit its contents, such as text.

Layer tool: Draw and position layers on a page as you would draw frames in InDesign. Hold down Command (Mac) or Control (Windows) as you drag on the edge of a layer to reposition it.

Grid Text Box tool: Draw and position text boxes on a layout grid. The Grid Text Box tool hides underneath the Layer tool.

Eyedropper tool: Sample a color from text or an object on a page and apply it elsewhere using this Adobe standard tool. Click and then drag to actively sample a color from anywhere on your screen.

Hand tool: Pan around your document quickly using this Adobe standard tool.

Zoom tool: Magnify a document up to 1600%. Drag a marquee around the area you want to focus on. Hold down Option/Alt and click to zoom out. Double-click the Zoom tool to revert to 100% view.

#52 Designing with Layers

For years, designing your Web pages using layers was a lot like trying to use hydrogen in your gasoline-propelled car. Web layout applications would write a bunch of excess code for browsers that barely supported layers. Well, times have certainly changed. These days most modern browsers include superior support for layers, and visual layout tools such as GoLive CS2 can now write the minimal amount of code required to render them.

Layers in GoLive are essentially HTML-based DIV tags accompanied by the requisite CSS needed to position them anywhere on the page. GoLive enables you to draw layers, resize and position layers, and not worry about the underlying source code (**Figure 52**). GoLive dynamically recodes the page with every change you make to the layer while keeping the source code as lean as if you coded it by hand. It's the truest sense of a visual layout Web editor.

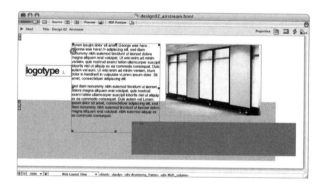

Figure 52 Layers in GoLive behave much like frames do in InDesign. You can drag and position them anywhere on your page. Layers can even overlap each other. You can finally lay out your pages however you want without being constrained by table cells.

If you want to add a layer in GoLive, you have a few options available to you:

- Use the Layer tool (see #51) to draw a layer box on your page.

- Drag the Layer icon ⬚ from the Basic Objects set in the Tools palette and drop it directly onto a page (or within an element on the page).

- Choose an insertion point by clicking a location on your page (for example, in another layer). Then click the Create New Layer button in the Layers palette (Window > Layers).

Once you add a layer to your page, a small yellow marker ⬚ appears representing the insertion point of the layer. To embed a layer within another layer, drag this marker into the other layer box. One of the key benefits of using layers is that you can easily resize or position them using the Object Selection tool. You can also assign a background color or an image to a selected layer using the Inspector palette. To add content to a layer, drag an object or asset into it or start typing into it using the Standard Editing tool. When you preview your page, the layer and its contents should appear exactly as you laid them out.

Using Split Source View

If you're curious to see the code GoLive generates when you add or edit a layer or any other object, switch to Split Source view by choosing View > Show Split Source. This is an excellent way to start learning to code for the Web by simply watching GoLive work.

#53 Working with CSS Layout Objects

Navigating CSS Layout Objects

If you're finding it difficult to select certain CSS layout objects you've nested in other objects, try using the Select tab of the Table & Boxes palette. Click the Select Parent Table button to navigate up to the parent object. A gray box represents a nested object that you can navigate down to by clicking on it.

Using CSS to lay out your Web pages offers many more benefits than traditional HTML-based layouts. The underlying code is leaner, maintenance is easier, and sites become more accessible. But laying out pages from scratch with CSS involves learning the complexities and somewhat esoteric rules related to the language. Fortunately, GoLive CS2 introduces CSS layout objects that make laying out pages with CSS as easy as dragging boxes onto a page.

CSS layout objects are prebuilt bits of CSS that GoLive works with intelligently. You simply drag a layout object onto a page and adjust its parameters via the Inspector palette. Layout objects are liquid designs, meaning parts of them stretch to accommodate the full width of the viewer's browser window. They are also modular, like interlocking toy building blocks. You can drag a layout object into another to quickly build up what would otherwise be a complex layout you would have to code by hand.

To start using CSS layout objects in your pages, follow these instructions:

1. From the Objects palette (which is now also the Tools palette), select the CSS set from the menu (**Figure 53a**).

Figure 53a Switch to the CSS set from the Tools/Objects palette to access the CSS layout objects.

2. Choose one of the CSS layout objects. Their icons suggest the type of layout they provide, but you can also hover over an icon with your pointer to get a tool tip containing a more informative description.

3. Drag the CSS layout object icon onto your page. You can also double-click the icon to automatically insert it to wherever your insertion point is on the page.

4. Nest CSS layout objects by dragging them into other objects such as separate layers (see #52) or even other CSS layout objects. For example, you can drag a Navigation Rows object into a Two Columns: Fixed Left object (**Figure 53b**).

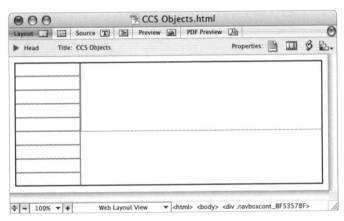

Figure 53b CSS layout objects make it easy to build up a CSS-based layout by nesting the objects in one another.

(continued on next page)

#53: Working with CSS Layout Objects

5. Edit the parameters of a selected CSS layout object you've placed on a page by opening the Inspector palette. Here you can adjust a layout object's column width, row height, padding, or overall height depending on the layout object selected (**Figure 53c**).

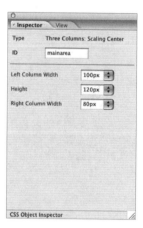

Figure 53c Once you place a CSS layout object on your page, you can edit its parameters via the Inspector palette.

6. Drag images or other site assets into your CSS layout objects just as you would any other container object in GoLive. Enter text by clicking into a layout object box using the Standard Editing tool.

#**54** Exploring the CSS Editor

Just as GoLive offers both visual and source-code editing tools to design your Web pages, the enhanced CSS Editor in GoLive CS2 gives you a choice of editing your stylesheets using a graphical user interface or switching over to the CSS code. You can even preview your stylesheet definitions directly from the editor without having to open a page and apply them.

To open the CSS Editor click the Open CSS Editor button 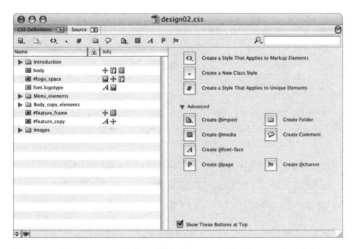 in the upper-right corner of a page in Layout mode. Once the CSS Editor is open, you'll notice that the right panel offers buttons with helpful explanations of the different types of items you can add to your stylesheet (**Figure 54a**). Miniature versions of these buttons will always display at the top of the editor if you select the Show These Buttons at Top option.

Figure 54a The right panel of the CSS Editor provides buttons for all the items you can create in your stylesheet.

If you create a new style definition or select an existing style, the right panel changes to show a set of icon-based tabs sorted into various categories of available styling properties. Use these tabs to find and add the properties you want to create your style.

(continued on next page)

Managing Styles with Folders

Using folders, GoLive provides an easy, familiar way to organize your styles when there's too many of them to keep track of. Click the Create folder button in the CSS Editor to add a folder to your set of styles. Name the folder and drag styles into it just as you would any other folder. Style folders are merely comments formatted in a way that GoLive knows how to treat them. Web pages will recognize them as standard CSS comments.

After you've added a property to a style definition, a representative icon for the property section appears in the Info column to the right of that style so you can see at a glance what's been defined. Click an icon to jump to its corresponding property tab.

You can preview styles while you're defining them by clicking the Show/Hide Style Preview button 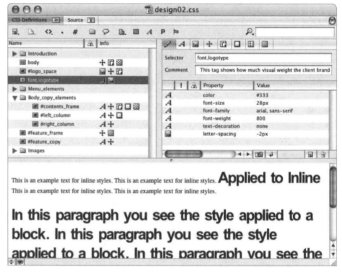 located in the bottom-left corner of the editor. This view gives you a good idea of the appearance of your style before you apply it to a page element and load it in a browser (**Figure 54b**). What a huge timesaver.

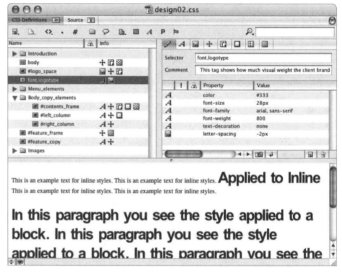

Figure 54b The Style Preview pane shows you an example of the selected style before you apply it to one of your pages.

In addition, if you're a code junkie or aspiring to become one, click the Show/Hide Split Source button ⬍ to view or edit the underlying code. You can also click the Source tab at the top of the editor window to switch entirely to code editing mode. Like all source views in GoLive, code completion is available, making it almost as much fun to define a style by hand (**Figure 54c**).

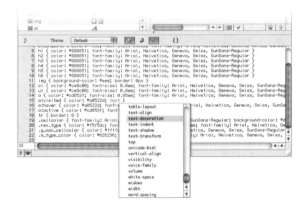

Figure 54c GoLive's code completion feature handles CSS as well as HTML.

#55 Applying CSS to Markup Elements

When applying CSS to markup elements, there are usually a handful of elements you find yourself styling again and again. The improved New dialog (File > New) offers a basic CSS file with many of these elements in it. In the New dialog , click the Web side tab and then select the CSS section to find this basic CSS file along with a slew of other CSS sample files. New sites include this basic CSS file by default.

When designing with Web standards in mind, it's always best to use semantically correct HTML tags before you start creating a bunch of unnecessary classes or ID selectors. This means that, among other things, you should wrap paragraph text in P tags and use H1 tags (or other header tags) for header text. You can then define a style that reformats the default appearance of the markup elements however you want. Not only does this result in cleaner, leaner code, but it makes your pages more accessible to viewer's who can't use your stylesheets for one reason or another.

Follow these steps to apply CSS to a markup element:

1. Open the CSS Editor (see #54) for your Web page or open your external CSS file.

2. Click and hold the New Markup Element Style button <>. . Select an element from the menu that appears (**Figure 55a**). For example, you could select the P tag for paragraph text. The new element style is added to your list of style definitions on the left, and the property section tabs appear on the right.

   Note: *If you don't see the element you want to apply CSS to in the element style examples menu, release the menu, click the New Markup Element Style button, and enter the element's name once it's created.*

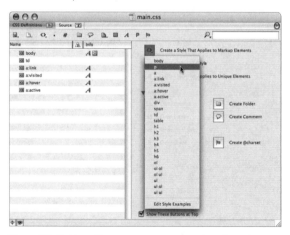

Figure 55a GoLive offers a great starter set of markup elements that you'll more than likely want to use and reformat.

3. Now assign any properties to your element style by clicking through the property section tabs and finding the properties you'd like to add. For instance, you could click the Font Properties tab and assign a different color, size, and font family set to your element style (**Figure 55b**). Click the Show/Hide Style Preview button to see your edits in action.

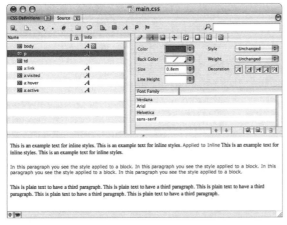

Figure 55b You can reformat any markup element you choose and then use the markup elements on your pages. This prevents you from creating an undue number of class styles.

4. Switch back to your Web page and try out your new element style. Add the HTML element for which you've created an element style. You can apply paragraph and header tags to selected text by using the Paragraph Format menu located on the far left of the Main toolbar. Once you add the element to your page, it should assume the appearance you've defined in its style.

#56 Using the Markup Tree Bar

Although GoLive offers an assortment of tools and palettes for selecting elements on a page and applying styles to them, none quite match the simple elegance and convenience of the Markup Tree bar. It's one of those tools that once you start using it, you'll wonder how you ever got along without it.

The Markup Tree bar is at the bottom of a document window in the Layout, Frame, and Outline editors. As you select an object within a page, notice how the Markup Tree displays the path of HTML tags, starting from the document's root tag to the element you have selected. This is great way to get a sense of where the element lives within the document hierarchy. But that's not all. You can click any of the tags along the path to quickly and precisely select the start and end tags along with their contents. You can also click and hold a tag in the bar to display a menu of the next lower level elements in the HTML hierarchy to select from (**Figure 56a**).

Figure 56a Click and hold a tag in the Markup Tree bar to display a menu of the next level of elements you can quickly select. Once selected, you can be confident that you're affecting the entire element when performing actions such as moving or deleting it.

You can use the Markup Tree bar for more than just selecting elements. If you Control-click (Mac) or right-click (Windows) a tag within the bar, a contextual menu pops up with a complete set of useful commands. From this menu, you can apply a CSS class or ID to a tag in one fell swoop (**Figure 56b**). This menu also offers handy commands for duplicating, deleting, and moving elements.

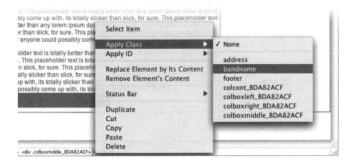

Figure 56b You can quickly apply a style to an element via the Markup Tree bar's contextual menu.

#57 Working with the Outline Editor

Unique to GoLive, the Outline Editor serves as a powerful yet easy-to-understand view into your Web page designs. The Outline Editor tab is situated between the Source Code Editor tab and the Preview tab. Within the Outline Editor you can see the HTML elements that make up your page in a hierarchical, structured view. Easily navigate through this structure by expanding and collapsing tags (**Figure 57a**).

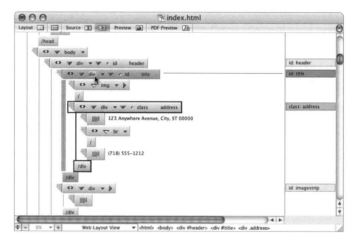

Figure 57a The Outline Editor provides a nicely structured view into your Web pages that can be less daunting than peering into the source code.

Attributes assigned to an element are displayed on their own level within the structure, making it easy to distinguish an attribute from an element. Finding available attributes and adding them to an element is just as easy. Simply expand a tag and select an attribute from the attribute menu by clicking the smallest down arrow directly to the right of the tag name (**Figure 57b**). This is useful when you don't exactly know which attributes are available for a particular tag or what they're referred to as.

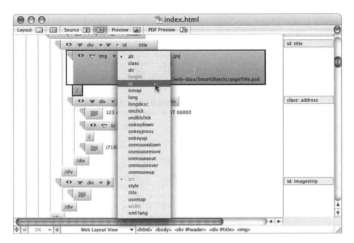

Figure 57b The attributes menu displays all the available attributes for a given tag, taking the guesswork out of which attributes you can choose.

You add elements to the Outline Editor just as you would in the Layout Editor. Drag elements from the Tools/Objects palette into a position in the structure to add them within the Outline Editor. Drag the gripper handle of a tag to move it to another location in the outline.

The Outline Editor is also effective at weeding out bugs in your pages since any broken links or syntax errors are highlighted in red, making them easy to notice and fix within one cohesive view (see #60). Be sure to click the Show Link Warnings button in the Main toolbar to have broken links highlighted.

#57: Working with the Outline Editor

#58 Using Live Rendering

One of the more tedious processes to go through when building your Web site is having to stop every so often after making a change to preview your results. Sure, sometimes you have to launch an actual Web browser to truly test your pages' compatibility, but at times switching to Preview mode in GoLive will suffice. But even switching to Preview can disrupt your normal workflow a bit. This is where Live Rendering comes in handy. Think of the Live Rendering window as a stand-alone Preview window that allows you to constantly preview your work while in any of the editors.

To open a page in a Live Rendering window, choose File > Preview In > Live Rendering. You can also use the keyboard shortcut Command+T (Mac) or Control+T (Windows). Once your page is loaded in the Live Rendering window, you can test aspects of your page such as CSS rendering, rollovers, and links, just as you can in Preview mode (**Figure 58a**).

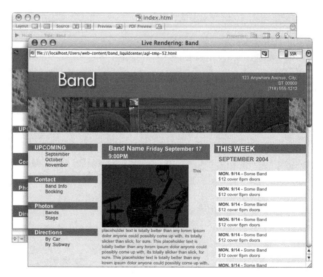

Figure 58a The Live Rendering window allows you to keep an eye on what your changes will look like without switching to Preview or an actual browser.

Live Rendering goes beyond Preview mode in some ways. Whenever you make a change to the underlying page, Live Rendering automatically updates to reflect that change. This feature is on by default, but you can verify that it is by clicking the Live Rendering window menu located in the top-right corner of the window and ensuring that the Auto Update option is indeed checked. You can also have multiple Live Rendering windows open at once. By default they will all update to display the currently active document (the frontmost window). But you can have a Live Rendering window bind to one document: select the document you want to lock the preview to and then choose Bound from the Live Rendering window menu (**Figure 58b**).

Figure 58b You can bind a Live Rendering window to a specific page by choosing Bound from the Live Rendering window's menu.

Adobe has also incorporated many features into GoLive CS2 with consideration to building pages that work as well on mobile devices as they do on computers. The Live Rendering window includes one of these features. You can click the Small Screen Rendering button ▢SSR to preview what your page will look like on a handheld mobile device, such as a cell phone or PDA.

#59 Adding a Favorite Icon to a Page

Favorite icons (or favicons) are the little custom icons that appear next to the address of a Web site or in the bookmarks or Favorites of your browser (**Figure 59a**). Although favorite icons are prevalent throughout the Web, they've been complicated to create and add to your Web pages. You had to track down specialized software to produce the uncommon image format (.ico) and then unearth the proper code required to integrate the icon into your page. GoLive CS2 simplifies this process with its introduction of Smart Favorite Icons.

Adding a Favorite Icon Site-wide

Although you can add a favorite icon to individual pages, you can just as easily add it to your entire site. Most modern browsers will look for a favorite icon file named "favicon.ico" in the root directory of a site. Knowing this, you can select your icon in the SmartObjects folder, choose Site > Smart Objects > Create Smart Favorite Icon, and save your exported file to the root of your site using the expected filename.

Figure 59a Favorite icons are located next to a Web site's address in many modern browsers. They're often used to reinforce the branding of the site and help as a visual cue after you bookmark a page.

Follow these steps to add a favorite icon to a page:

1. Create your icon in Photoshop or Illustrator at 16 x 16 pixels. GoLive doesn't resize the image icon when it's created so it's best to work in the typical size of favorite icons in Photoshop. Opt for simple, clear shapes for your icon since their small nature make subtle details hard to distinguish.

2. When you've finished creating your icon, click the Extras tab of the Site window and save the file in the SmartObjects folder.

3. In GoLive, open the page you want to add the favicon to and drag the Smart Favorite icon from the Smart Objects set in the Tools/Objects palette to the page. GoLive recognizes that this belongs in the header of the page so it conveniently places the icon there for you.

4. With the Smart Favorite icon selected in the page header area, go to the Inspector palette. Drag the Fetch URL (aka the pick whip) 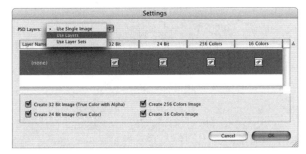 and point it at your new icon in the Smart-Objects folder in the Site window.

5. The Settings dialog opens (**Figure 59b**). Here you can save various versions of the icon at different bit depths. If you've designed your icon in Photoshop, you can choose to use individual layers or layer sets (now known as layer groups in Photoshop CS2). Click OK to continue.

Figure 59b The Smart Favorite Icon Settings dialog lets you choose to use a single image, layers, or layer sets (layer groups) from a Photoshop file as your icon.

6. GoLive keeps the name of your icon file but appends the required .ico file extension. Choose a location to save the exported .ico file and then click Save. The icon is now represented in the Smart Favorite icon in the page header.

7. Now all you have to do is upload your Web page and favicon file to your server. You can also try to temporarily preview the page in a browser as you normally would: choose File > Preview In > *your favorite browser*. Firefox shows the favicon in action but other browsers may not display the icon until you've posted it to your site and browsed to it from there.

#60 Checking the Syntax of Source Code

Whether you take advantage of GoLive's visual layout tools or feel comfortable editing in source code mode, mistakes can still occur in the code. These unfortunate accidents can result in visitors to your site not being able to view a page, having the page render in a weird way, or causing page functionality to break. Just as it's crucial to preflight your InDesign document before handing it over to a printer, it's as important to check for syntax errors throughout your site before going live with it. But don't worry; you're not on your own with all this. GoLive can locate these issues, inform you of what's going wrong, and help you to quickly fix these errors.

To check the syntax of an open page, do the following:

1. Choose Edit > Check Syntax or click the Check Syntax button ⚡ if you happen to be in the Source Code Editor or Split Source Code mode.

2. In the Check Syntax dialog that appears (**Figure 60a**), decide which document type or types to comply with. Leaving !DOC-TYPE assigned selected is usually a safe bet, especially if you've created your site in GoLive CS2, which now by default creates pages as XHTML Transitional. This document type is what many consider the standard these days. Click OK to start the syntax check.

Figure 60a
You can select the document type (or types) the Syntax Checker should comply with from this dialog.

3. The Check Syntax Results window will appear if the Syntax Checker finds any issues on your page. From this window you can see the number of issues found and where they're located (element, line number, and column). Although you can see the errors and fix them in any editor, I suggest switching to the Outline Editor (see #57) for viewing and fixing problems in a unified view.

4. In the Outline Editor you can scroll through the page and see all issues highlighted in orange with a bright yellow box containing the explanation of the error beside it (**Figure 60b**). You can also select an issue in the Check Syntax Results window, if you still have it up, and go directly to its location on the page.

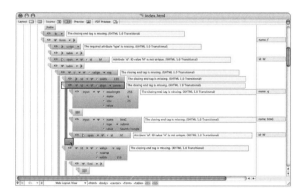

Figure 60b The Outline Editor is ideal for displaying syntax errors and correcting them.

5. Once you've attempted to fix all the issues on the page, go to the View palette (usually grouped with the Inspector palette) and click the Highlight tab. Click the Rescan button to rebuild the highlighted results to make sure you haven't missed any errors.

To check the syntax of an entire site, choose Edit > Check Syntax with no pages open or selected in the Site window. If you want to check the syntax of certain pages in your site, select them in the Site window and then choose the Check Syntax command.

#60: Checking the Syntax of Source Code

CHAPTER SEVEN

Creative Suite Integration

So this is where Adobe's decision to bring the products together into one suite really comes to fruition. The very word, suite, can't be attached to software without people expecting an incredible level of integration between the products that's never been realized before. Happily, Adobe has met the expectation with Creative Suite 2. Very few other software companies have enjoyed this kind of interoperability among their applications as Adobe has. Whether you're bringing Illustrator artwork into Photoshop or considering how to take your InDesign document to GoLive, the Creative Suite is there to answer the call.

With CS2, you can move your creative elements freely between the applications while maintaining a considerable amount of editability. Have a Photoshop file you'd like to integrate and continue to work with in Illustrator? No problem. Do you want to turn off a layer in your placed Photoshop file without leaving InDesign? Sure, why not? These are the types of features and capabilities a suite promises, and without question CS2 delivers.

Here are some of my favorite integration points within the suite. They mainly focus on bringing elements of a document over into another CS2 application while keeping (or sometimes even gaining) as much flexibility as possible as you move forward in your workflow.

#61 Bringing Illustrator Artwork into Photoshop

Placing Illustrator Files

With the advent of Smart Objects in Photoshop CS2, Illustrator files placed into Photoshop (File > Place) are automatically converted into a Smart Object layer (see #25). This is smart (sorry) since you can then freely resize the placed file without having to worry about the rasterized image degrading. Placing your Illustrator file makes sense when you have an elaborate piece of artwork you'd like to continue to edit as a stand-alone file in Illustrator. Double-click the Smart Object layer thumbnail of the placed file to edit it in Illustrator. Once you save your edits, the Photoshop file automatically updates.

The tight integration that exists between Illustrator and Photoshop makes it possible to bring your Illustrator artwork over to Photoshop and continue to work with it. You have a few different options available to you with each offering and varying degrees of continued edibility of your artwork. Although some of these options have been mentioned in earlier techniques, it makes sense to cover all the bases in one place.

Pasting artwork

Pasting Illustrator artwork into Photoshop is best suited for times when you want to transport bits of simple artwork and continue to edit them. When you paste artwork into Photoshop, the Paste dialog asks you which format you'd like the artwork to be pasted as: Smart Object, Pixels, Path, or Shape Layer (**Figure 61a**).

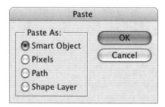

Figure 61a The Paste dialog in Photoshop CS2 presents you with four options to choose from for how your artwork comes in.

Here's a brief explanation of the results of each option:

- **Smart Object:** Selecting Smart Object embeds the artwork within the Photoshop file as a Smart Object layer. You can continue to edit the embedded artwork in Illustrator by double-clicking the Smart Object layer thumbnail. When you save and close the artwork, the Smart Object is updated in Photoshop. Note that pasting artwork as a Smart Object breaks its association to the original Illustrator file you created it in. Consider placing the file instead of pasting it if you'd like to maintain this link.

- **Pixels:** Pasting as pixels is the most clear-cut and probably the most limiting of the set of options. Your vector artwork is rasterized and inserted as a normal layer into Photoshop. If you resize the artwork afterwards, the rasterized image starts to degrade.

- **Path:** Selecting Path pastes your artwork as a path that can then be selected via the Paths palette and edited with the Pen and Direct Selection tools.

- **Shape Layer:** Pasting as a Shape Layer results in your artwork coming over as a single shape layer (see #24). Photoshop will even leave your compound shapes intact (see #34). Pasting as a shape layer is ideal when you want to continue to edit your artwork as vector artwork in Photoshop using its tools.

Exporting as a Photoshop file

If you'd like to bring your entire Illustrator file into Photoshop while keeping elements such as layers, transparency settings, and editable text intact, consider exporting it as a Photoshop file. With your Illustrator file open, choose File > Export in Illustrator and then select Photoshop (.psd) from the Format menu. Decide on a name and location for the exported file and then click the Export button. You will be prompted with the Photoshop Export Options dialog (**Figure 61b**). In this dialog, determine the color mode and resolution you want to save the Photoshop file as and keep the Write Layers option selected along with its editability suboptions. Click OK to export your Illustrator file. Open the exported file and notice that all your layers and blending modes are just as they were in Illustrator. You can even edit text since it comes over as type layers. How's that for integration?

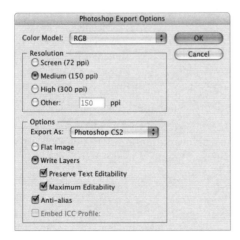

Figure 61b The Photoshop Export Options dialog in Illustrator CS2 is your one-stop shop to get your artwork into Photoshop with layers, text, and other attributes intact.

#61: Bringing Illustrator Artwork into Photoshop

#62 Making a PDF Presentation from Photoshop Layer Comps

Changing Page Transitions

If you're not happy with the presentation's default page transition, change it within Acrobat Professional. With your PDF presentation open in Acrobat Professional, select Document > Set Page Transitions and choose from 40 different transitions. You can also adjust the timing of the transitions from this dialog.

Photoshop's layer comps really come in handy when you want to explore different creative avenues in your design. Nothing beats being able to flip through several comps within the same document so that you, your colleagues, or client can review different approaches and decide among them. But what if it's not possible to get everyone huddled around your screen? Not a problem. Just save your set of layer comps as an Acrobat PDF presentation so that everyone can review and comment on them from the comfort of their own computer.

Here's how to make a PDF presentation from your layer comps:

1. In Photoshop, open the document that has the desired set of layer comps created within it (see #73).

2. Choose File > Scripts > Layer Comps To PDF. A dialog appears prompting you to choose a destination for the resulting Acrobat file (**Figure 62a**).

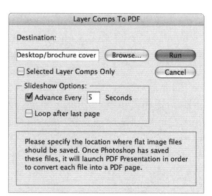

Figure 62a Use the Layer Comps To PDF dialog to set the options for your exported PDF presentation.

3. If you just want to select specific layer comps to save to the PDF file, be sure to first select the comps you want in the Layer Comps palette (**Figure 62b**) and then check the Selected Layer Comps Only option in this dialog. You can opt to adjust the available Slideshow Options for advancing the pages after a certain number of seconds and looping after the last page.

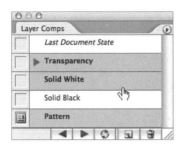

Figure 62b Hold down Command (Mac) or Control (Windows) to select multiple, noncontiguous layer comps. Then you can choose to export only those selected layer comps in your presentation.

4. When you're ready to create the PDF presentation, click the Run button. Once Photoshop has flattened and packaged all your layer comps, Acrobat launches and opens the presentation in full screen mode for you to preview. Each layer comp becomes a slide in the presentation. Press the Escape key to exit full screen and stop the presentation.

5. Now you can send the PDF presentation out for feedback via email or for download from your file server or Web site.

#63 Importing Photoshop Files into Illustrator

What's Not Imported

Unfortunately, some Photoshop layer features aren't supported in Illustrator and will get flattened (merged and rasterized) in the conversion process. The unsupported layer features are adjustment layers, most layer effects, clipping masks, and some blending modes: Dissolve, Color Dodge, Color Burn, Difference, Linear Burn, Linear Dodge, Vivid Light, Linear Light, and Pin Light. Illustrator does its best to preserve the appearance of these features by flattening the layer with underlying or affected layers.

Not to be outdone by Photoshop's ability to bring over Illustrator artwork (see #61), Illustrator includes exceptional support for importing Photoshop files. Among Illustrator CS2's import options is the ability to select layer visibility or a layer comp within a Photoshop file. You can even choose to convert the Photoshop layers to objects and editable text where possible.

Follow these steps to access these import options when placing or opening your layered Photoshop file in Illustrator:

1. Make sure your Photoshop file (.psd) is ready to import into Illustrator—that is, you no longer need to edit it in Photoshop.

2. Within Illustrator, choose File > Place. Locate your Photoshop file and select it. If you want to import the actual Photoshop objects directly into your Illustrator document, be sure to uncheck the Link option in the Place dialog. Then click the Place button. You can also open a Photoshop file via Illustrator's Open command to place the file in a new Illustrator document.

3. The Photoshop Import Options dialog offers you a set of import options (**Figure 63**). In Illustrator CS2, you can select a particular layer comp to import if your Photoshop file happens to have one. If you checked the Link option in the Place dialog, the When Updating Link menu will be available to you to decide which layer settings are honored: Photoshop's or the settings you changed within this dialog. In the Options section you can choose to either Convert Photoshop layers to objects or Flatten Photoshop layers to a single image. (The Flatten option is your only option if you decided to link the file.) If your Photoshop file includes hidden layers, image maps, or slices, these options will become available to you as well for import. Choose between the two main import options (convert or flatten) and click OK.

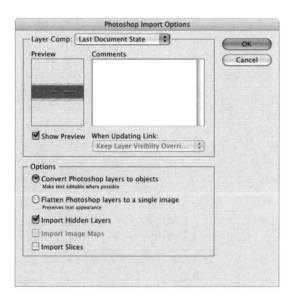

Figure 63 The new Photoshop Import Options dialog in Illustrator CS2 allows you to select a layer comp from your Photoshop file.

4. If you opted to convert your Photoshop objects, you'll notice that practically everything translates over from Photoshop. Layers, layer groups, most blend modes, opacity settings, masks, and even text come through intact. Now you can continue to work with the objects in Illustrator as if you created them there.

Importing PDF Files into Illustrator

Illustrator has been speaking Acrobat's language (PDF) for a number of versions now. So not only are Illustrator files really just PDF files with additional information (try opening an Illustrator [ai] file in Acrobat and see what happens), but Illustrator has no problem opening a PDF file no matter what application produced it. This means you can take a PDF generated from InDesign or QuarkXPress and open it directly in Illustrator to edit it. The one downside is that all the text will be broken up into individual sets of letters instead of selectable as words and paragraphs.

#64 Saving Out Multipage PDF Files from Illustrator

Some argue that you should do your page layout in a page layout application (say in InDesign), not in a drawing application. But many purists and resourceful users have continued to use the classic page-tiling feature found in Illustrator to create multiple pages in their documents. Although you've always been able to print out tiled documents (otherwise what's the reason for them), the challenge remained as to how to easily produce a multipage PDF from them. In Illustrator CS2, Adobe has thankfully made this possible.

Here's how to save your tiled Illustrator document as a multipage PDF:

1. In Illustrator, choose File > Print, and in the General set of options in the Media area of the Print dialog, select the page size you want the resulting PDF pages to be.

2. Select Setup in the options list on the left side of the dialog. Keep the Crop Artwork to menu at the Artboard option. In the Tiling menu, choose either Tile Full Pages or Tile Imageable Areas (**Figure 64a**). Select Tile Full Pages to make Illustrator separate the artboard into as many whole pages as will fit, resulting in no partial pages being displayed or printed. Select Tile Imageable Areas to divide the artboard into as many sections needed to print all the artwork. Click the Done button.

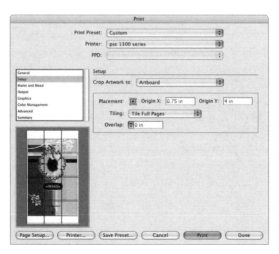

Figure 64a
Choose either Tile Full Pages or Tile Imageable Areas from the Setup page of the Print dialog.

3. Set up your Illustrator document so the artboard can accommodate the number of pages you want in it by choosing File > Document Setup and entering the artboard dimensions. For example, a four-page letter document could be tiled on a 17 x 22" artboard.

4. Choose View > Show Page Tiling to see the tiling divisions on the artboard. You can use the Page tool 🔲, which is the hidden tool under the Hand tool, to adjust where the tiling divisions lie on the artboard.

5. When you have your tiling set up and your artwork in place, you can save it as an Acrobat file. Choose File > Save a Copy, and then in the Save a Copy dialog select Adobe PDF (.pdf) from the Format menu. Decide on a name and location for the PDF and click Create. In the ensuing Save Adobe PDF dialog, check the Create Multi-page PDF from Page Tiles option (**Figure 64b**). Notice that you can't preserve Illustrator editing capabilities with this option selected. This is why I suggest saving a copy instead of saving your native Illustrator file.

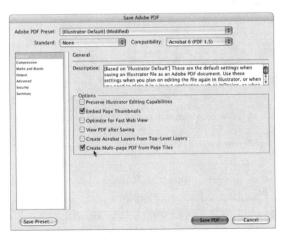

Figure 64b To export your Illustrator file as a multipage PDF, you must check this option in the Save Adobe PDF dialog.

With your multipage PDF file saved, you can then send it to others to print from Adobe Reader or Acrobat Professional. And the best part is, your recipients won't even know you used a drawing application to lay out your multiple pages.

#64: Saving Out Multipage PDF Files from Illustrator

#65 Changing Layer Visibility of Placed Photoshop and PDF Files in InDesign

InDesign now allows you to selectively toggle the layer visibility of placed PSDs and PDFs, but alas not native Illustrator (ai) files. To overcome this limitation, save your Illustrator files in the Adobe PDF format. In the PDF Options dialog, choose Acrobat 7 Compatibility and select Acrobat Layers from Top-Level Layers. As long as you keep the Preserve Illustrator Editing Capabilities option selected, the PDF file will remain editable just like a native Illustrator file but allow you to change layer visibility when placed in InDesign.

InDesign CS2 offers a long sought-after integration feature: the ability to toggle layers on and off within placed Photoshop and PDF files. This means you can adjust the visibility of any layer in InDesign without jumping over to Photoshop or Acrobat Professional. The layer visibility in the original file isn't altered, so you can in effect use one linked file that appears different with each placement of it. If your placed Photoshop file includes layer comps, you can switch between them as well.

To set the layer visibility of a placed Photoshop or PDF file, select the placed file in your InDesign document. Then choose Object > Object Layer Options. Within this dialog (**Figure 65a**), you'll find a portal into all the layers in your Acrobat or Photoshop file as well as the layer groups and layer comps of your Photoshop file. You may want to select the Preview option, although this can get sluggish with larger files.

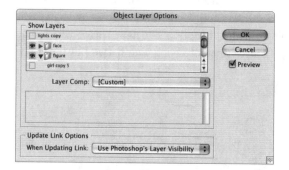

Figure 65a A long wished-for feature has found its way into InDesign CS2. You can now selectively toggle the visibility of layers in your Photoshop and PDF files directly in InDesign.

Click any layer or layer group eye icon to hide a layer just as you would in Photoshop. To show a layer or layer group, click the empty eye box next to it. Drag through the eye column when you want to adjust the visibility of multiple layers at once. If you've placed a Photoshop file that contains layer comps, you can choose between them from the Layer Comp pop-up menu.

Another setting to consider is the When Updating Link option (**Figure 65b**). If you want InDesign to always match the layer visibility set in the linked file, select the Use Photoshop's/PDF's Layer Visibility option. This means that if you go back to the linked file and change the layer visibility, InDesign will then use these updated layer visibility settings once the link is updated. If you want to always keep the layer visibility settings you've designated in this dialog, select the Keep Layer Visibility Overrides option. Click OK and watch with amazement as your placed file magically updates (if you didn't have Preview selected, that is).

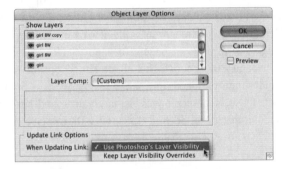

Figure 65b Use the When Updating Link menu to specify which layer visibility should be honored: the linked file or the settings in InDesign.

#66 Placing Multipage PDF Files in InDesign

In #64, I explained how Illustrator saves a multipage PDF from your tiled document. Now let's say you're feeling somewhat embarrassed about using Illustrator for your page layout needs and decide you want to bring the multipage PDF into InDesign—or any multipage PDF for that matter (it doesn't have to be from Illustrator). Fortunately, Adobe has made it possible to place multiple-page PDF files into InDesign CS2.

Choose File > Place. To let InDesign know you want to place more than just the first page of your multipage PDF file, you must select Show Import Options in the Place dialog (**Figure 66a**). With this option selected, you'll be presented with the Place PDF dialog (**Figure 66b**). Within the Pages section of the dialog, you can choose to place the page you're currently previewing in the Preview section, all pages, or a range of pages. To import multiple pages from your multipage PDF, choose the All or Range option. The Range text field supports specifying pages to import as a range using a hyphen (1-3), separate pages using commas and spaces (1, 3, 8), or a combination of both (1-3, 7). Click OK to place your PDF pages.

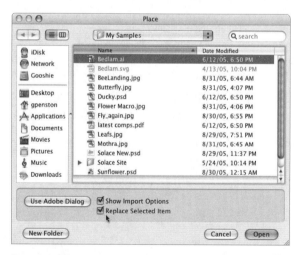

Figure 66a When placing your multipage PDF, be sure to check Show Import Options in the Place dialog to display the Place PDF dialog.

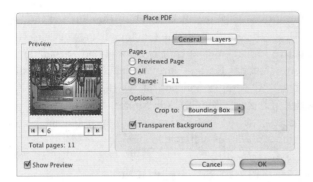

Figure 66b The Place PDF dialog lets you specify which pages of a multipage PDF you would like to place.

After you click OK in the Place PDF dialog, your cursor changes to the loaded multipage PDF icon. Click anywhere in your document to place the first page you've specified to import. Notice that after you place the PDF page, your cursor remains a loaded icon. InDesign reloads the cursor with the next page ready for you to place. Place the second page on the current page or navigate to another page to place it. You can even create new pages via the Pages palette: Your PDF pages stay loaded in the cursor while you navigate and create your pages. Continue this process until all the pages you've specified in the PDF are placed. If at anytime you want to cancel the placement of the remaining pages in your cursor, click the Selection tool.

Place Multiple Pages at Once

When placing a multipage PDF, it usually makes sense to place pages one at a time so you can jump to other pages in the document or add new pages as needed. But if you want to just place all the pages at once, hold down the Option/Alt key once your cursor is loaded. The cursor will then change to a loaded multipage PDF stacked icon. Click anywhere in your document, and all of the remaining pages in your PDF will be placed at once, stacked on top of one another.

#67 Building an Interactive PDF in InDesign

Sure, InDesign is a page layout application through and through, but it turns out to be a very capable tool for getting your ideas into an interactive format. Among InDesign's well-known page layout tools are less familiar features for creating interactive PDF files. You can create hyperlinks and bookmarks that result in navigational aides in the exported PDF. You can also add buttons to your InDesign document and then assign actions such as jumping to a page, playing a movie, or hiding elements.

Adding bookmarks and hyperlinks

You can add bookmarks to your InDesign document to make it easier navigate the exported PDF. The bookmarks appear in the PDF within the Bookmarks tab in Acrobat or Adobe Reader (**Figure 67a**). To create a bookmark, open the Bookmarks palette in InDesign by choosing Window > Interactive > Bookmarks. Next, decide where you want the bookmark to jump to by clicking an insertion point in text, highlighting text, selecting a graphic, or choose an entire page by double-clicking on a page in the Pages palette. Then just click the New Bookmark button on the Bookmarks palette to create the bookmark.

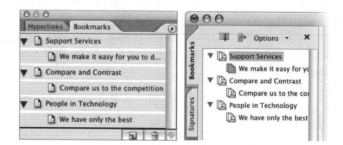

Figure 67a Bookmarks that you create in your InDesign document (left) end up in the exported PDF (right), making it easy for readers to navigate your document.

Hyperlinks are similar to bookmarks but allow you to set up navigational links directly within your document's content much like a Web page. Adding and managing hyperlinks is all done in the Hyperlinks palette (Window > Interactive > Hyperlinks). Select

Using Hyperlink Destinations

Text anchors require that you set up a hyperlink destination first by choosing New Hyperlink Destination from the Hyperlinks palette menu. Setting up hyperlink destinations is a good idea for pages as well, especially if you're still shuffling the pages around. If a page moves in your document, you only have to update the hyperlink destination instead of several hyperlinks that directly point to a specific page.

the text or graphic you want to act as your hyperlink's source and then click the New Hyperlink button in the Hyperlinks palette. In the New Hyperlink dialog (**Figure 67b**), name your hyperlink and choose a destination. Destinations can be other pages (even in other documents), a URL (e.g., www.adobe.com), or a text anchor. You can then choose an appearance for your hyperlink and click OK. When you export your PDF, be sure to select the Include Bookmarks and Hyperlinks option in the Export PDF dialog.

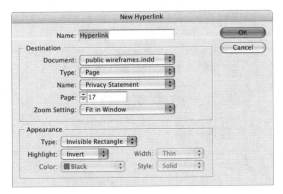

Figure 67b Use the New Hyperlink dialog to specify a destination and appearance for your hyperlink.

Creating buttons

You can create buttons in InDesign and set them up to perform actions when the document is exported to a PDF. You can create a button by using the Button tool to drag out an area on top of text or a graphic. (A button acts as an overlay, so you still need to create content for your button.) But the easiest way to create a button is to select your button content (text or graphics) and choose Object > Interactive > Convert to Button. Once you've created your button, you can then assign actions to it by choosing Object > Interactive > Button Options. In the General tab, you can edit the name, description, and visibility attributes of the button. Switch to the Behaviors tab of the dialog (**Figure 67c**) to add

(continued on next page)

Advanced Button Techniques

If you want to show or hide an element, make it a button first and then create another button with the behavior Show/Hide Fields. This behavior allows you to toggle the visibility of any other buttons in your document. You can also add your buttons on master pages for behaviors like previous and next page, so you don't have to repeatedly add them to your pages. Buttons can also have rollover states. Choose View > Interactive > States to bring up this palette to add rollover and down states to your buttons.

Placing Movie and Sound Clips

You can place movie and sound clips into your InDesign documents just as you'd place any type of supported graphics file. QuickTime 6 or later is required to place QuickTime, AVI, MPEG, and SWF movie clips, and WAV, AIF, and AU sound clips. Although the clips can't be played in InDesign, they can be exported in a PDF and played in Acrobat Professional or Adobe Reader. You can even create buttons to play the media.

behaviors triggered by certain events. For example, to show the next page in your document when you click the button, you would choose Event: Mouse Up along with Behavior: Go To Next Page. Remember to click the Add button in the lower-right corner of the dialog to add the behavior you've set up. To make your buttons function in your exported PDF, select the Include Interactive Elements option in the Export PDF dialog.

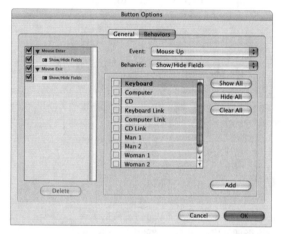

Figure 67c The Button Options dialog offers several useful behaviors that you can associate to common events like mouse clicks and rollovers.

#68 Packaging InDesign Documents for GoLive

Let's say you've laid out your document in InDesign and then want to reuse many of the graphics and text in a GoLive site. Before the Creative Suite this practically meant starting over again to move all the elements into formats suitable for online viewing. But now InDesign and GoLive go together like peanut butter and jelly. InDesign collects all your text stories and graphics in your document, converts them into Web-friendly formats, and outputs it all into a nice package that you can then load into your GoLive site and start working with.

Use the following steps to package your InDesign document for GoLive:

1. With your document open in InDesign, choose File > Package for GoLive.

2. Decide on a name and location for the package. If you already have a GoLive project site set up that you'd like to add the package to, save it to the web-data\InDesignPackages folder of that site's project folder. If you don't have a site set up, you can always move the package in later; save it to wherever you'd like for now. Once you've selected a location and named your package, click the Save button.

3. After you click Save, a Package for GoLive dialog appears with options organized into three sections (**Figure 68**).

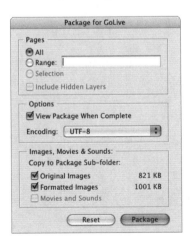

Figure 68 The Package for GoLive dialog in InDesign makes it simple to select which pages and assets should be packaged together.

Original vs. Formatted

The copy images options in the Package for GoLive dialog are somewhat vague in their distinctions: Original Images vs. Formatted Images. Select Original Images to copy the original images in your document to the package so that you gain the flexibility to optimize them directly within GoLive. If you have images that have been cropped or transformed and you'd like to retain these settings, select the Formatted Images option to have InDesign copy a set of images with this formatting applied. For ultimate flexibility in GoLive, select both options.

Packaging Books

In #50, I explained how to work with InDesign's handy Book feature. If you've taken advantage of this feature and want to export your book as a package, you can. From the Book palette menu, choose Package > Book for GoLive and then choose a location for the package and select your options.

- In the Pages section, you can decide to package all the pages in your document, a specific range, or just the objects you currently have selected. If your InDesign document includes hidden layers, you can select the Include Hidden Layers option to package those objects as well.

- In the Options section, check the View Package When Complete option to have the package open in GoLive afterwards. And unless you're working on a multilingual site, you can leave the encoding option set to UTF-8.

- The Images, Movies & Sounds section offers the option to copy the original and formatted images along with any movies and sounds you may have in your document to a subfolder in the package.

3. Click the Package button. InDesign begins to process your document. Text stories are converted to XML files for easy GoLive digestion, placed images and graphics are converted to TIFF images, and paragraph and character styles are translated into corresponding CSS for GoLive. Depending on the complexity and size of your document, package creation may take a while. After InDesign has processed your document, your newly created package is ready to work with in GoLive.

#69 Working with InDesign Packages in GoLive

Once you've successfully saved your InDesign document as a package, you're ready to work with it in GoLive. You open an InDesign package in GoLive by double-clicking on it. The package then opens in a separate window in GoLive where you can quickly browse and zoom in on assets, and then drag them into your working GoLive page. Here's a rundown of how to get up and running with the package window.

- **Highlighting, tool tips, defaults:** Hover over items with your mouse in the InDesign Layout tab, and the bounding box of the item will highlight in green. Wait a second and a tool tip will appear providing details about the item. Items appended with TextFrame will result in HTML text by default when dragged onto a page (**Figure 69a**), whereas anything else will result in a graphic by default.

Figure 69a Hovering over a page in a package window will highlight the item in green and eventually display a tool tip with details about the item.

- **Adding text or tables:** To add text or a table to your GoLive page, simply drag the item from the InDesign Layout tab in the package window onto your page. You have three options available to you as to how the text should be inserted: Smart Component, Editable Text, or Snapshot Image. You choose the insert option of a text item before you add it to your page by clicking it in the InDesign Layout tab and then open the Inspector palette. You then choose one of the options from the Insert As menu (**Figure 69b**):

(continued on next page)

Updating InDesign Packages

Since all assets placed from InDesign into GoLive result in Smart Objects by default, you can experience the power of this feature firsthand when you perform changes within the InDesign document. Make any changes you need to in the InDesign document. Select Package for GoLive as before and point to the location of your original package. InDesign should then ask if you want to update the package. Click Update and once the update is complete, all the assets that you placed in your GoLive site as Smart Objects update automatically.

Figure 69b With a text frame selected in the package window, you can open the Inspector palette to decide on the format the text should be inserted as.

Editable Text: With the Editable Text option, you can directly edit the inserted HTML text in GoLive, but you lose any formatting or automatic updating from InDesign.

Smart Components: By default, text frames and tables are inserted as Smart Components. Smart Components have a dynamic link back to the source InDesign document, allowing the text and formatting to automatically update when the package is updated. But this means you must go back to the InDesign document to edit the text or rely on GoLive's XML editor.

Snapshot Image: The Snapshot Image inserts the text frame as a Smart PDF object. A Smart PDF creates an image file from the text, allowing you to preserve any unusual fonts or formatting the text may have that can't be reproduced reliably in HTML alone. And since Smart is in its name, yep, you guessed it, it will automatically update when the InDesign package is updated.

- **Adding an image or graphic:** To add an image or graphic, drag the object from your package window to your page. All images and graphics dragged from your package window are Smart Objects (see #70) by default. As with text frames, you can click on an image or graphic in the InDesign Layout tab and then open the Inspector palette to adjust the asset conversion settings (**Figure 69c**). In the Inspector palette you can select the Use Image With InDesign Formatting setting to keep any formatting you may have applied such as clipping paths, cropping, and borders (provided you saved your package with this option). You can also select an optimization preset from the Web Format menu.

Figure 69c When inserting graphics, you can jump to the Inspector palette to decide whether to use the InDesign formatting of the image or graphic along with the optimization setting.

#70 Using Smart Objects in GoLive

Update Matting via Drag and Drop

If the source file you're using as a Smart Object has a transparent background and you choose to change the background of your Web page to something other than white, you'll probably notice an undesirable white fringe (known as matting) around your Smart Object. To quickly remedy this issue, choose Special > Page Properties and open the Inspector palette. Drag the color swatch from the Background color well to your Smart Object and drop it on top. Your Smart Object's matte color now matches your page's background and the white fringe is eliminated.

Although Smart Objects can now be found in Photoshop as well, they originally made their appearance in GoLive. Smart Objects in GoLive eliminate the need to optimize your Creative Suite documents into Web-friendly formats before bringing them into GoLive. You can drag a Photoshop, Illustrator, or Acrobat file into a document in GoLive to make it a Smart Object. GoLive creates a dynamic link between the source file and the resulting Web-optimized files. Smart Objects make it easy for you to freely transform and edit the source files without having to resave the optimized files every time you make a change. GoLive automatically re-creates these files for you on the fly.

You can import your source files (native CS2 documents) and have them live anywhere in your GoLive project site folder. However, Adobe sets up a specially designated folder at web-data\SmartObjects just for storing all your source files in one place. You can find this special folder in your site window by toggling Split View and clicking the Extras tab (**Figure 70a**).

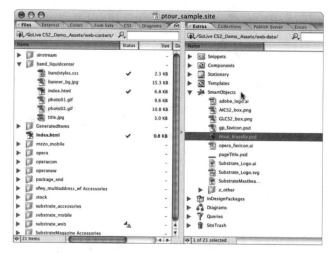

Figure 70a You can add all your native source files to the SmartObjects folder in the Extras tab of your GoLive site project folder. You can then access them easily from there or the Library palette's Smart Objects tab.

Once you have your source files in your GoLive site, you can easily drag them from the SmartObjects folder into a GoLive document. GoLive then displays its very own Save for Web window so you can decide on the optimization settings and where the optimized files should be saved. GoLive creates a dynamic link between the source file and the resulting Web-optimized files and updates the page with the resulting image. Now you can resize the Smart Object without worrying about the image degrading since GoLive goes back to the source to reoptimize. You can edit the source file by simply double-clicking on the Smart Object within the page. After you've saved any changes to a file, GoLive automatically updates to reflect the changes to the Smart Object. If you want to edit the optimization setting of your Smart Object, select it and open the Inspector palette (**Figure 70b**). In the Basic tab, click the Settings button to call up the Save for Web window again.

Figure 70b With your Smart Object selected, open the Inspector palette to adjust any of its optimization settings.

Smart Objects offer more than just automated image optimization. This merely scratches the surface of the flexibility and power Smart Objects bring to Web design in GoLive. Be sure to take advantage of them. Once you do, you'll never want to be without them.

Slices in Smart Objects

GoLive's Smart Objects support slices from Photoshop, ImageReady, and Illustrator. Note that Illustrator files must be saved in the SVG file format with the Include Slicing Data option selected in the Save dialog to have Illustrator slices read into GoLive. Just create your slices as you normally would and drag the source file into GoLive. GoLive then saves a data folder with the optimization settings and all the generated images. Now if you decide to adjust your slices, the Smart Object will automatically update.

#70: Using Smart Objects in GoLive

CHAPTER EIGHT

Designing for Creative Flexibility

Change is good. Or at least that's what they say. But I don't think they were talking about changes from clients at the eleventh hour. In those situations, change isn't so good; it's actually kind of troubling. But if you've done your homework and set up your Creative Suite documents properly to account for these sorts of last-minute changes, you may well greet them with the utmost conviction and take them on instead of dreading them.

Another kind of change is when you decide to head off in a different design direction. You shouldn't feel stifled by your software when creative inspiration strikes. Being able to explore many creative directions in your designs should only be limited by your time and inspiration, not your software.

This chapter focuses on the features and tools found throughout the Creative Suite that help manage last-minute changes and allow you the freedom to easily go off in a completely new design direction without losing where you began.

#71 Using Adjustment Layers in Photoshop

Selectively Applying an Adjustment

If you want to apply an adjustment layer to just a portion of your image, add a mask to the layer (see #22). Painting with different tones of gray permits you to control how much of the adjustment is applied. You can also change the adjustment layer's opacity from the Layers palette to selectively control how much of the adjustment is applied overall.

Adjustment layers in Photoshop allow you to make color and tonal adjustments to an image without permanently changing the underlying pixels. This nondestructive method of editing means you can try different modifications to an image at any time by editing the adjustment layer. For example, instead of applying the Levels command to your file and hoping it prints out acceptably once it's saved and placed in InDesign, you can add a Levels adjustment layer that provides the flexibility to go back later and change the Levels settings if necessary. Adjustment layers also reduce the loss of image data since you're not applying multiple adjustments directly to the image over time.

Creating adjustment layers is easy, and they increase your file size no more than any other layer. So it's hard to come up with a good reason for not taking advantage of them. To quickly create an adjustment layer, click the New Fill or Adjustment Layer button at the bottom of the Layers palette and then select any of the 12 adjustment commands available in the pop-up menu (**Figure 71a**). All the standard favorites are available: Levels, Curves, Hue/Saturation, and so on. The appropriate adjustment dialog will then pop open for you to apply your edits. These dialogs are the same as the ones you're used to seeing that directly apply to the image. Make your adjustments as you normally would and click OK.

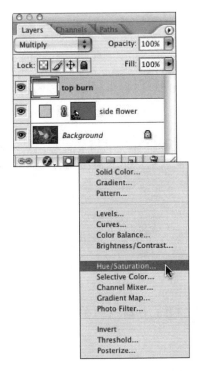

Figure 71a The adjustment layer pop-up menu located in the Layers palette gives you quick access to creating an adjustment layer.

The adjustments are applied and then represented as a layer in the Layers palette (**Figure 71b**). Since it's a layer, you can do almost everything you can do to image layers: toggle visibility, reorder the layer in the stacking order, apply a mask, and so on.

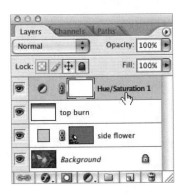

Figure 71b Once an adjustment layer is applied, it appears in the Layers palette. Each adjustment command is represented by a different thumbnail icon.

(continued on next page)

#71: Using Adjustment Layers in Photoshop

Here's where it gets interesting. To edit an adjustment layer, simply double-click the adjustment layer's thumbnail in the Layers palette. The adjustment's dialog opens again, allowing you to tweak any settings and reapply them. You can edit an adjustment layer at any time, even after you've saved and reopened the document.

Note: *You can apply and edit adjustment layers only in Photoshop, although you can view them in ImageReady if the document's color mode happens to be in RGB.*

#72 Working with Layer Styles in Photoshop

Layer styles let you add to a layer an array of live effects that automatically update whenever the layer's content changes. For example, you can apply a drop shadow to a type layer, and the drop shadow will automatically update as you change the text of the layer. Similar to adjustment layers, layer styles are nondestructive, so you can return to them at any time to edit existing effects or add new effects to the style without degrading the quality of the image.

To apply a layer style to a selected layer, click the Layer Styles button at the bottom of the Layers palette and choose an effect from the pop-up menu. The Layer Style dialog (**Figure 72a**) opens and offers options for the effect you selected. Be sure to select the Preview option so you can see the effect in action on the layer. It's also a good idea to set your view at actual pixels (100%) so the effects appear as they actually will in print once applied. Make any other adjustments to the default settings and click OK. You can apply other effects while in this dialog by selecting any of the effect names in the list that appears on the left.

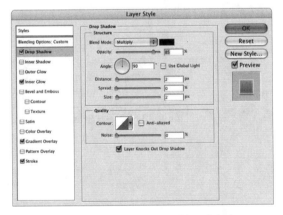

Figure 72a The Layer Style dialog provides all the layer effects and settings in one easy to manage interface.

(continued on next page)

Dragging to Adjust Layer Effects

While in the Layer Style dialog with the Preview option enabled, you can use the Move tool to directly drag the previewed effect around on the canvas to adjust its settings. For example, when applying a drop shadow, you can drag the shadow interactively, right on the canvas. About half of the layer effects support this form of direct manipulation: Drop Shadow, Inner Shadow, Texture, Satin, Gradient Overlay, and Pattern Overlay.

Using Layer Styles with Rollovers

Although layer styles are useful in any situation, they really shine when setting up button rollovers in ImageReady. Using only layer styles you can have a single layer define the various rollover states of a button by toggling the visibility of the layer effects. This is where layer effects such as Color Overlay, Gradient Overlay, Stroke, and Outer Glow really come in handy.

Once you've applied your layer styles to a selected layer, they appear indented below the layer in the Layers palette (**Figure 72b**). Notice that a small "f" icon ⓕ appears to the right of the layer name. This indicates that layer effects are applied in case you collapse the layer effects list by clicking the triangle beside the icon. You can easily edit an effect by double-clicking it. And just like layers, you can toggle the visibility of a layer effect by clicking the eye icon next to the effect. Click the eye icon next to the top-level Effects row to toggle all the effects of a layer on and off. To copy an effect to another layer, simply drag it to that layer. To move an effect, hold down Option/Alt while dragging. You can also store and apply layer styles via the Styles palette much like you manage color swatches from the Swatches palette.

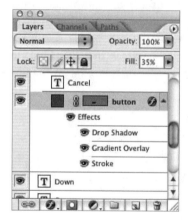

Figure 72b A layer style's effects are indicated directly below the layer. Click a layer effect eye icon or the Effects eye icon to toggle its visibility on and off.

#73 Creating Layer Comps in Photoshop

If you've fallen into the habit of creating multiple design compositions or comps in a single Photoshop file and then turning its layers on and off to review the different design directions, layer comps are definitely going to make your day. Layer comps save the current state of all the layers in the Layers palette, capturing the visibility, position, and appearance of the layers. A layer's appearance is based on the layer styles applied (see #72) and its blending mode.

To create a layer comp, make sure the layers are visible and positioned along with their appearance set to how you want the layer comp to be captured. Open the Layer Comps palette (Window > Layer Comps), which by default resides in the palette well. In the Layer Comps palette, click the New Layer Comp button. In the resulting dialog (**Figure 73a**), supply a name for your layer comp and decide which layer settings should be captured and applied to the layer comp. You can optionally add a comment to the layer comp that then appears below the layer comp name once it's created. Click the OK button to finish creating your layer comp.

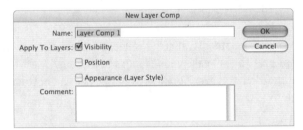

Figure 73a When you create a layer comp, you have the option of capturing the visibility, position, and appearance of the layers in your document.

Now one layer comp isn't really that useful, since there's nothing to switch back and forth between, so continue to create other layer comps by turning on and off layers and their styles, and repositioning them. Then click the New Layer Comp button again and follow the previous detailed steps.

(continued on next page)

Duplicating Layer Comps

Although it may not be apparent at first, you can drag a layer comp to the New Layer Comp button to duplicate it. Once it's duplicated, you can then make slight variations to the layer's settings and update the duplicated layer comp to become a new design direction for the image.

Exporting Layer Comps

Once you've created your layer comps, you can easily share them with others by exporting them. You can export your layer comps as individual files, a PDF presentation (see #62), or a Web photo gallery (WPG). Choose File > Scripts to access all three layer comps export options.

Once you have a couple of layer comps created, you can start viewing them via the Layer Comps palette (**Figure 73b**). Click the empty box to the left of a layer comp name to view it. The Apply Layer Comp icon 🔳 will then appear in the box. You can click the Previous and Next Selected Layer Comp buttons ◀ ▶ at the bottom of the Layer Comps palette to cycle through all the layer comps. If you first select certain layer comps by Command-clicking (Mac) or Control-clicking (Windows) them, the buttons will cycle through only your selected set.

Figure 73b Use the Layer Comps palette to quickly and easily flip through different comps by either clicking the empty gray box next to a layer comp name or using the left and right arrows at the bottom of the palette.

If you want to update a layer comp, select the layer comp in the Layer Comps palette and make your changes to the layer's settings. Then click the Update Layer Comp button 🔄 at the bottom of the palette.

Note: You can also create layer comps in ImageReady. Illustrator and InDesign now allow you to select a layer comp when placing a Photoshop file that contains them (see #63 and #64).

#74 Working with Graphic Styles in Illustrator

You can rely on graphic styles to quickly and consistently apply a set of appearance attributes to your artwork in Illustrator. It's a one-click operation that changes the fill, stroke, transparency, and effects of objects. If you or your client decide to change one of these attributes later on, just update the graphic style and all the elements with the style applied update along with it.

To apply a graphic style to a selected object or group, open the Graphic Styles palette (Window > Graphic Styles) and click the style you want to apply (**Figure 74**). Graphic styles can also be applied via the Control palette or simply by dragging the style from the palette and releasing it on top of an object.

Figure 74 Graphic styles in Illustrator make it possible to take an ordinary shape and turn it into a compelling element with one click.

To create a graphic style from your own design, build up your object with any combination of appearance attributes. Use the Appearance palette to add multiple fills and strokes, and manage any effects you apply (see #37). To add the object's appearance attributes as a style just drag it directly into the Graphic Styles palette. Now you can apply the style to any other objects in your document. Use the Save Graphic Style Library option in the Graphic Styles palette menu to save your styles as a library file so you can load them into other Illustrator documents. Graphic styles are saved with the document they were created in.

You can update a graphic style by replacing the attributes used in the style. The simplest way to do this is to create an object you'd like to use to replace the style and then hold down Option/Alt while dragging the object on top of the graphic style in the Graphic Styles palette. This redefines the style with your new appearance attributes, and any occurrences of the original style will automatically update.

Merging Graphic Styles

You can create a new graphic style from two or more existing graphic styles by merging them. This new graphic style will contain all the appearance attributes found in the styles it was based on. Command-click (Mac) or Control-click (Windows) to select multiple styles and then choose Merge Graphic Styles from the Graphic Styles palette menu.

Exploring the Libraries

Be sure to explore all the preset graphic styles that ship with Illustrator. Not only are these great to experiment with, but they're also worthwhile to deconstruct using the Appearance palette to learn what's possible when using appearance attributes. You can find these graphic style libraries in the Graphic Styles palette menu under the Open Graphic Style Library option.

#75 Using Paragraph Styles in Illustrator and InDesign

Do Away with Double Returns

We all know that we're not supposed to add two spaces after punctuation when using these new-fangled computers, right? Well, you can also do away with adding double returns for imposing space between paragraphs. Instead, use a single return to end a paragraph and then use the Space After formatting option 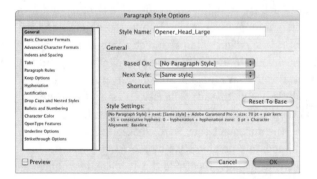 in the Control palette to set a specific amount of space between your paragraphs. Define this in your paragraph style in the Indents and Spacing area, and you gain ultimate control of the space between your paragraphs throughout your entire document.

Paragraph styles in Illustrator and InDesign make it possible to apply a consistent set of character and paragraph formatting attributes to a paragraph or several paragraphs at once. Then when you change any of the formatting attributes in the paragraph style, all the paragraphs in your document with the applied style automatically update. Paragraph styles are essential for laying out documents consistently while incorporating the flexibility for changes later on.

Although you can create a paragraph style completely from scratch, it's much more straightforward to first apply all the formatting you want to include in your style to a paragraph of text. Once you have the formatting applied to the paragraph, click the New Paragraph Style button in the Paragraph Styles palette while holding down the Option/Alt key. (To access the Paragraph Styles palette, choose Window > Type in Illustrator or Window > Type & Tables in InDesign.) You will then be able to rename your paragraph style and make any adjustments to the formatting attributes within the Paragraph Style Options dialog that opens (**Figure 75a**). Enable the Preview option so you can immediately see what effect any changes you make to the style will have without exiting the dialog. Once you're satisfied with your paragraph style, click OK. With your paragraph style created, you can start applying it to paragraphs within your document.

Figure 75a The Paragraph Style Options dialog is your control center for defining all the formatting attributes (both character and paragraph) that will comprise your paragraph style. Notice that the Style Settings provides a helpful summary of the formatting applied in your style.

You can apply a paragraph style via the Paragraph Styles palette in Illustrator or InDesign. InDesign also offers a Paragraph Style drop-down menu in the Control palette when you have it switched to the Paragraph Formatting Controls ¶ . You can also take advantage of the new Quick Apply feature (see #49) in InDesign. To activate Quick Apply, press Command+Return (Mac) or Control+Enter (Windows) and then start typing part of the style's name. When the name is highlighted, click Return or Enter again to apply the selected style. Since a paragraph style applies to an entire paragraph, you don't have to worry about selecting the whole paragraph before applying the style. Just have your text insertion point within the paragraph or select a portion of the paragraph you want to apply the style to. You can select any part of multiple paragraphs to quickly apply a paragraph style to all of them at once (**Figure 75b**).

Redefining Styles

As with object styles (see #48), you can redefine character and paragraph styles. Select text with the style applied using the Type tool. Then make any changes to the character or paragraph formatting attributes. Within the applicable Styles palette, choose Redefine Style from the palette's menu. Your style, as well as all text with the style applied, will instantly update with your changes.

Figure 75b You don't need to select an entire paragraph to apply a paragraph style to it. You can even select just portions of multiple paragraphs to quickly apply a style to them at once.

#76 Using Character Styles in Illustrator and InDesign

Using Both Style Palettes at Once

Using Both Style Palettes at Once

The default workspace settings in both Illustrator and InDesign have the Character and Paragraph Styles palettes grouped as a set. Sure, this helps save precious screen real estate, but it can sometimes be a pain to switch back and forth between the two frequently accessed palettes. Try docking (see #4) the Character Styles palette to the bottom of the Paragraph Styles palette so both are available at the same time.

If you want to consistently format certain characters, words, or sentences but not necessarily paragraphs, look no further than character styles. Character styles are available in Illustrator and InDesign, allowing you to establish a collection of formatting attributes that you can quickly apply to a selection of text (**Figure 76a**). And since it's a style, you can perform last minute formatting changes at, well, the last minute instead of frantically scouring through your document for the particular formatted bits of text to update.

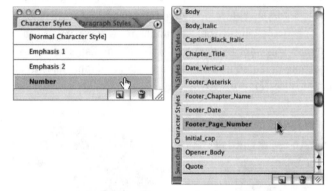

Figure 76a Illustrator and InDesign include character styles and their requisite palettes. Both applications' options and interfaces for creating character styles are virtually identical.

You can create character styles completely from the ground up by selecting the formatting options you want from the Character Styles Options dialog. With no text selected, click the New Character Style button in the Character Styles palette while holding down Option/Alt to start a new style from scratch. (To access the Character Styles palette, choose Window > Type in Illustrator or Window > Type & Tables in InDesign.) You can also base a character style on formatting you've already applied to existing text. Using the Text tool, select the portion of text that includes the formatting you want to base your character style on. Then click the New Character Style button. Once you've created your character style, you can begin applying it to other selections of text throughout your document.

To apply a character style to a selection of text, click the style name in the Character Styles palette in Illustrator or InDesign. In InDesign, you can also select the style from the Character Styles drop-down menu in the Control palette (**Figure 76b**) when you have the Character Formatting Options mode selected A or call up the Quick Apply panel and start typing part of the character style's name.

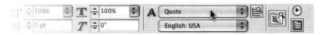

Figure 76b InDesign's Control palette provides quick access to your character styles. This is convenient if you happen to be working in the Control palette anyway.

#77 Defining Character Styles with Paragraph Styles in Mind

Preserving Character Styles and Removing Overrides

If you have text selected that you want to apply a paragraph style to and preserve character styles but remove any stray formatting (overrides), hold down Option/Alt while clicking on the paragraph style name in the palette to apply it. To remove both the character styles and overrides, hold down Option/Alt+Shift while applying the paragraph style.

Character styles can contain as much or as little formatting as you want to assign to them. This is important to consider when defining your character styles, especially if you want them to play well with other paragraph styles you've created.

For example, you could create a character style to use for emphasis based on existing text. The character style might specify the font family, font style, size, leading, and color formatting attributes (e.g., Myriad, bold, 10 point over 12, and red) (**Figure 77a**). Although it is perfectly fine to specify this level of formatting in a character style, you may find that it causes some formatting headaches when applying the character style within text that also has a paragraph style applied.

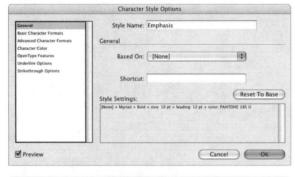

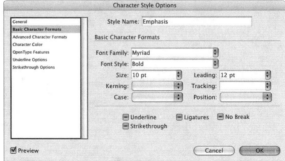

Figure 77a You can define as many character formatting attributes as you want in your character style, but it may complicate matters later on when paragraph styles are also applied.

But let's say you know the character style will coexist with paragraph styles that already determine the font family, size, and leading. So all you really need to specify in the character style is the font style and color (bold and red) (**Figure 77b**). If you then decide to change the paragraph style's font family (say from Myriad to Warnock Pro), your character style perfectly adapts to apply just the additional formatting attributes required to emphasize the text (bold and red). Using character styles in this manner, to only override formatting attributes that have already been specified in the paragraph styles, really taps into the powerful flexibility character styles can offer.

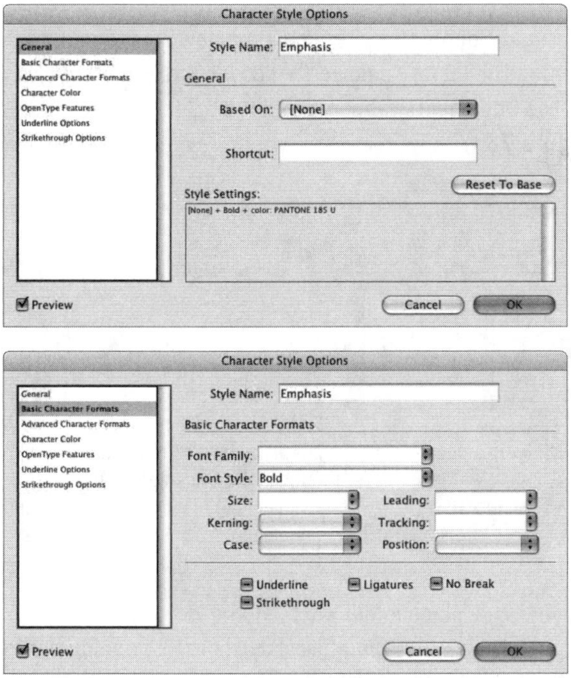

Figure 77b Defining just the formatting attributes necessary to override what's already been defined in paragraph styles is far more flexible to changes in both.

#78 Working with Components in GoLive

Components in GoLive are blocks of your Web pages that you can reference within multiple pages throughout your site and then have them automatically update whenever a component is changed. Components behave similarly to Smart Objects in GoLive (see #70) but instead of helping with graphic-based source files, they help you manage chunks of HTML code that are susceptible to changes and may appear on several pages in your site. This makes components ideal for headers, footers, mastheads, and other common navigation elements that would be tedious to update on every single page of your site.

Follow these steps to create a component source file and then use it in other pages:

1. With your GoLive site open, create a new component page by opening the Library palette (Window > Site > Library), choosing the Documents tab, and double-clicking Component Page (**Figure 78a**).

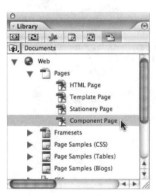

Figure 78a Although you can use any HTML page as a component, using the Library palette's preset component page in the Documents tab is an uncomplicated way of creating your component.

2. Remove the placeholder text on the new component page and add any content you like. For example, you could add all the links that appear in the footer of your site. You needn't worry about linking your external stylesheet (CSS) to the component page since the component will ultimately exist in the actual pages the CSS is applied to. GoLive will also contend with reconciling links to other pages in the site once the component is added to them.

3. Save the component page (File > Save As) to the Components folder of your site. GoLive targets this location (web-data\ Components) when the Save As dialog opens because you started with a preset component page.

4. Once the component is saved, you can start using it in other pages in your site. To add your component to a page, drag it from the Components tab of the Library palette onto the page (**Figure 78b**). Components are also available in the Extras tab of the site window.

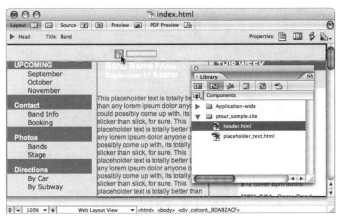

Figure 78b To add a component to a page, drag it from the Components tab of the Library palette onto the page.

5. Add the components to one or more pages within your site. To update a component, just double-click it in any page where it's been added. Make any changes to the component, and once you save them, all the pages where the component has been added will automatically update.

Cropping Text in Components

GoLive CS2 lets you crop text in components you've added to your pages. You can use one component to create several instances, all cropped differently. With a component selected in the Layout Editor, open the Inspector palette and click the Crop Text button [T]. Then select the text you want to keep in the component or jump to the Main toolbar to specify a certain amount using the Crop Text By menu. When you're ready to apply the crop, click the Accept Crop button in the Main toolbar ✓.

#79 Changing Photoshop Layers in a GoLive Smart Object

Updating Variable Settings

Once you've added your Photoshop Smart Object with variables to a page, you can update your variable settings by selecting the Smart Object and opening the Inspector palette. Click the Variables button in the Basic tab, and the Variable Settings dialog will become available to you once again to make any changes.

Smart Objects in GoLive offer you incredible flexibility in what you can do with native CS2 files dragged onto a GoLive page (see #70). Yet believe it or not, there's more. It's possible to change the text or visibility of layers in a Photoshop Smart Object right in GoLive.

If you create a Smart Object from a Photoshop file that has a type layer as its topmost layer, you'll be able to change the text in that type layer when you drag the file into GoLive. GoLive will prompt you with a Variable Settings dialog where you can click the Use check box and enter different text for the type layer (**Figure 79a**).

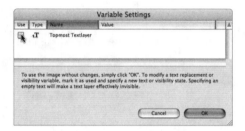

Figure 79a If your Photoshop file has a type layer as its topmost layer, GoLive will prompt you with this dialog when you drag the file onto a Web page.

If you'd like to gain this level of flexibility for lower-level type layers or the visibility of layers, you'll first have to define them as variables in Photoshop. But don't let the techie term put you off; variables are surprisingly easy to set up.

Here's how to set up variables in Photoshop for use in GoLive:

1. With your source file open in Photoshop, choose Image > Variables > Define.

2. In the Variables dialog (**Figure 79b**), choose the layer you'd like to define as a variable for from the Layer menu. Type layers offer visibility and text replacement options, whereas image layers offer visibility and pixel replacement options—although the pixel replacement option isn't pertinent to this technique.

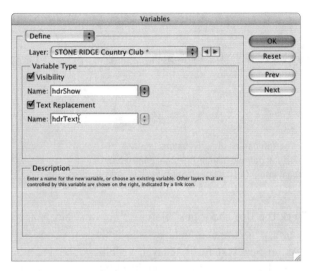

Figure 79b Use the Variables dialog to define which layers and their properties should become variables.

3. Select the options you'd like to enable and supply meaning-ful names for the variables. Make sure your variable names start with a letter and don't contain any spaces. You can use underscores (_) or change case to help separate words in your variable names.

4. Repeat this process for however many layers you'd like to be able to change in GoLive. When you're done, save the Photoshop file to your GoLive project site folder in the web-data\SmartObjects folder.

With your variables set in Photoshop, you can then see them in action:

1. In GoLive, drag your Photoshop file from the Smart Objects folder in the Extras tab of your site window onto a GoLive page. The Variable Settings dialog appears with all your defined variables (**Figure 79c**).

(continued on next page)

#79: Changing Photoshop Layers in a GoLive Smart Object

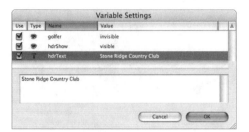

Figure 79c You can change the values of any variables you defined in your Photoshop file when you drag it into a GoLive document.

2. Check the Use check box related to any variables you'd like to adjust. Text replacement variables offer a text box for you to enter new text for that layer. Visibility variables provide you with a menu to toggle the visibility of that layer. When you're done adjusting the settings, click OK.

3. Decide on your optimization settings in the Save for Web window and choose a location for the optimized file. Your Photoshop Smart Object shows up on your page with the new text or visibility settings you've entered.

#80 Using CSS in GoLive

Much like character, paragraph, and object styles in InDesign make it effortless to change formatting of elements across an entire document, cascading stylesheets (CSS) allow you to make sweeping changes to text formatting and other properties across an entire site. But as with element styles in InDesign, it takes a little bit of foresight and discipline to realize the flexibility and nimbleness that using CSS affords.

For the ultimately flexibility within your site, every significant element should have some way to specify it in a style. This doesn't necessarily mean you need to create a slew of classes for each type of element found in your site. It just means you should have a way to style the element via the different kinds of selectors. Heavily peppering your site with inline styles not only makes it difficult to maintain a level of consistency but also makes it next to impossible to change these styles.

Here are a few pointers when using CSS to allow for the most flexibility for changes down the line and minimize the amount of additional code:

- **Create markup styles (HTML selectors) before resorting to classes and IDs.** Build your Web pages using semantically correct HTML tags (<p> tags for paragraphs, etc.) and style them however you want (see #55). Then use class (.) and ID (#) selectors for special formatting needed within the markup styles.

- **Move your internal styles to an external stylesheet when appropriate.** This prevents you from leaving inconsistent formatting in pages that you can't affect globally. You can export an internal stylesheet to an external stylesheet using the CSS Editor pop-up menu (**Figure 80**).

(continued on next page)

Descendant Selectors

You can specify a style for a particular element on a page just by referring to its relative tags above it in the HTML hierarchy. These are referred to as descendant selectors. For example, it's possible to create a style that pertains only to P tags that exist in a DIV tag with the ID of "sidebar" by creating a descendant selector like: #sidebar p {color: #333}. Once you get a handle on descendant selectors, you'll realize that you can further minimize the amount of additional classes and IDs in your CSS. Visit the W3C (www.w3c.org) to learn more about descendant selectors.

Figure 80 You can effortlessly export an internal stylesheet to an external one by using the Export Internal CSS command in the CSS Editor pop-up menu.

- **Take advantage of external stylesheets.** Not only do external stylesheets provide a means to centralize and manage all your styles in one location for quick editing, but they're beneficial to visitors of your sites as well. Browsers typically cache an external stylesheet, so they don't have to load the styles again when other pages are visited within your site.

- **Use CSS layouts and layers.** GoLive's CSS layout objects and CSS-based layers make it easy to design visually with CSS (see #53). CSS usually results in leaner code than older table-based techniques and offers you greater flexibility and options in terms of formatting and positioning.

CHAPTER NINE

Automating Routine Tasks

I'm still waiting for the day when my computer will do practically everything I ask of it with no complaints. Even though technology has advanced by leaps and bounds these last couple of decades, we are still slaves to our systems. Sure, it's gotten much better than it once was, but we still have to nudge, click, and enter commands into our computers for them to understand what we want from them. That's why I'm excited when I discover a way to get my computer to take over a rather tedious or monotonous task for me. This is as it should be, since computers handle routine tasks rather well, whereas it turns out, we humans do not.

The Creative Suite happens to offer a variety of features designed to automate tasks and eliminate tedium. If you find yourself trapped in a vicious cycle of performing the same actions over and over again in a CS2 application, saying, "There's got to be a better way," well, most likely there is. With a suite of applications this mature and versatile, you can often find a command or feature that will do the mind-numbing work for you. The challenge is to know where to look for them and understand how to use them.

In this chapter, I've compiled a collection of features and techniques that offload the heavy lifting onto the applications: these tasks include processing hundreds of files, creating galleries and contact sheets, automatically setting up rollovers, and more. As a result, you regain your free time so you can get back to what's most important—being creative.

#81 Crop and Straighten Photos in Photoshop

Although digital photography has become increasingly popular these days, you may still find yourself scanning in some old photo prints on your flatbed scanner. But having to crop and straighten each print afterwards has always been a pain. Well, we can put all this tedium behind us now and let Photoshop's amazing Crop and Straighten Photos command do the work for us. This remarkable command not only automates the process of cropping and straightening your photos for you, it can do so to multiple images within a single scan.

Follow the steps below to use the Crop and Straighten Photos command:

1. Place your prints on your flatbed scanner and scan them all in at once (**Figure 81a**). To get the best results, arrange your prints on the scanner bed so they are at least 1/8 of an inch apart from one another. It's also a good idea to disable any automatic adjustment settings your scanner software may offer since they often take into account the entire scanned image. You can always adjust the individual images in Photoshop once they've been cropped (and straightened) from the scanned file.

Figure 81a With the Crop and Straighten command, you can save time by scanning in several photos at once.

2. Open the scanned file in Photoshop. If you want to apply the Crop and Straighten Photos command to specific images in the scan, make a selection around them.

3. Choose File > Automate > Crop and Straighten Photos. Photoshop processes the scanned file, detecting the edges of each image, and then crops, straightens, and separates them into individual files (**Figure 81b**).

Figure 81b Once the Crop and Straighten command has worked its magic, you'll end up with a separate document window for each image.

4. With each image conveniently cropped and straightened for you, you can then make any adjustments to them (see #27) and save them as individual files.

#82 Using the Image Processor in Photoshop

Applying Settings from the First Image

If you're processing a set of camera raw files taken under the same lighting conditions or your source images' color profiles don't match your working profile, you can select the Open first image to apply settings option. This will give you an opportunity to adjust settings in the first image when it opens and have those adjustments applied to the remaining images being processed.

These days our computer hard drives are inundated with an over-abundance of images we offload from our digital cameras, download from stock photography services, or create ourselves. Processing all these images into different file formats or image dimensions can be daunting at best. Fortunately, Photoshop CS2 introduces the Image Processor, which processes multiple files. It performs many common image-related tasks so you don't have to create an action and use it within a Batch command.

Here's how to use the Image Processor:

1. In Photoshop, choose File > Scripts > Image Processor. The Image Processor window appears (**Figure 82**).

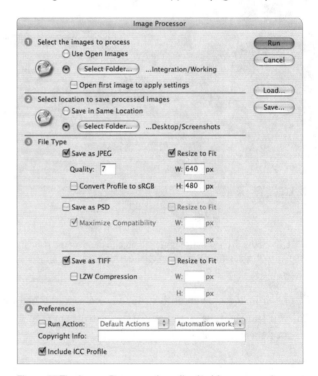

Figure 82 The Image Processor is well suited for common image handling needs where creating a Batch action would be overkill.

2. Select the image files you want to process. If you already have the images that you want to process open in Photoshop, select the Use Open Images option. Otherwise, click the Select Folder button and choose the folder that includes the images ready for processing.

3. Select the location where you want to save the processed files. You can save the files to the same location or choose a different folder.

4. Select the file types along with the options that you want the Image Processor to save (e.g., JPEG, PSD, TIFF). You can opt to convert your files into one of these formats or any combination at the same time. Selecting multiple formats at once will result in each type being saved when your images are processed. Selecting the Resize To Fit option will resize the images to best fit within the dimensions you enter while retaining their original proportions.

5. You can optionally set any of the other processing options. You can select a Photoshop action (see #84) to run or decide to include copyright information or a color profile within each image processed.

6. Click the Run button and the Image Processor will start working its magic. Your images will be saved to the destination you specified within folders named using the file formats you selected.

Processing Images via Bridge

Many of the Automate commands in Photoshop's File menu are also available from within Bridge. Image Processor just happens to be one of them. Select the images you want to process within Bridge and then choose Tools > Photoshop > Image Processor. The Image Processor window then opens in Photoshop, and the Images to process options area is changed to "Process files from Bridge only {selected count}."

#83 Creating a Web Photo Gallery in Photoshop

Adobe Stock Photos and Web Gallery

If you've found photos through the new Adobe Stock Photos service in Bridge (see #8) that you would like your client to evaluate, you can create a temporary Web photo gallery for your client to review. From the Adobe Stock Photos tab in Bridge, select all your photos and click the Download Comps button in the header. Once they're downloaded, switch to the Downloaded Comps tab, select your comps, and then create your Web photo gallery. Consider using the "feedback" gallery styles to make it easy for your client to comment on specific images. Also, make sure your gallery is temporary (meaning up for less than 30 days), private, and only for evaluation purposes.

Photoshop can automatically generate a completely interactive Web photo gallery from your images that you can then share with others via your Web site. Photoshop offers a variety of gallery styles to choose from; a couple are even Flash-based.

You can create a Web photo gallery either from Photoshop or Bridge. But by choosing Bridge to select your images, you can preview the images you're selecting as well as decide on the order in which they will appear in your gallery. Drag your images around in the Bridge window to change their order in the gallery.

With your images selected (and ordered) in Bridge, continue with the following steps:

1. Choose Tools > Photoshop > Web Photo Gallery. Photoshop opens and the Web Photo Gallery dialog appears (**Figure 83a**).

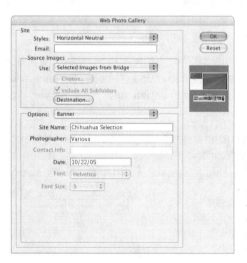

Figure 83a The Web Photo Gallery dialog is where you choose the gallery style along with other details, such as thumbnail size and gallery title.

2. Decide on a style for your gallery using the Styles pop-up menu. The thumbnail preview will update with the style you've selected. You can optionally add your email address, but keep in mind that doing so can result in unwelcome emails from spammers.

3. Since you selected your images from Bridge, you can skip the Use pop-up menu and go right to the destination for your gallery. Click the Destination button and select a location for the gallery to be saved.

4. Cycle through all the formatting options for your selected gallery style on the Options pop-up menu. With these options you can customize your gallery by adding a site name for your gallery, adjusting the size of the large images and thumbnails, and choosing any additional information about your photos that you want displayed.

5. Once you've selected the formatting options, click OK and Photoshop commences with the construction of your Web photo gallery. When Photoshop is done creating the gallery, the home page of the gallery will load into your browser so you can preview the results (**Figure 83b**).

Figure 83b When Photoshop is done generating your new gallery, the gallery will open in your browser so you can preview it.

6. You may want to repeat the creation of the gallery a few times to try different gallery styles and see them in action. The thumbnail preview is a bit too small and isn't as helpful as viewing the galleries in your browser. When you're happy with the gallery style you've selected, you can post your gallery to your Web site using GoLive or your favorite FTP application.

#83: Creating a Web Photo Gallery in Photoshop

#84 Using Actions in Photoshop and Illustrator

Conditionals in ImageReady

I would be remiss if I didn't mention that ImageReady shares the same Actions features found in Photoshop. In fact, ImageReady goes one better than Photoshop by offering conditionals. Look for the Insert Conditional option on the Actions palette menu in ImageReady. You can use conditionals to test a condition and assign the steps to take if the condition is met. You can even nest actions by using conditionals. Let's hope Photoshop includes these soon.

If you find yourself performing the same task over and over again in Photoshop or Illustrator, it's probably high time you take a couple of minutes and create an action to handle the task for you. Actions are a sequence of commands that you can record and repeatedly play back on a file or a batch of files.

To start working with actions, open the Actions palette (Window > Actions) (**Figure 84a**). A set of default actions is available in both Photoshop and Illustrator for you to start experimenting with. If the Default Actions folder set is collapsed, click the triangle to expand it and reveal the actions it contains. You can expand each action to expose its steps. You can load other sample actions from the Actions palette menu. Deconstructing the sample actions is a great way to learn just what's possible with actions.

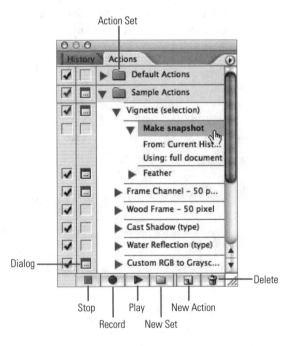

Figure 84a The Actions palette houses just about everything you need to create and manage actions.

To play an action, select it and click the Play Selection button at the bottom of the Actions palette. If any of the steps in the action has a dialog icon ▣ next to it, you'll be greeted with a dialog. This allows you to enter custom values each time the action is run. You can click a dialog icon to toggle it off. A red dialog icon indicates one or more of the steps in the action have dialogs enabled, whereas a dark gray dialog means all the steps have dialogs turned on. You can also omit steps of an action by drilling into them and unchecking the check mark icon beside the step you want to skip. Actions can be represented in the palette by buttons by choosing Button Mode in the palette's menu. You can then click the button of the action to play it.

To create an action:

1. Click the New Action button at the bottom of the palette.

2. In the New Action dialog box (**Figure 84b**), name your action and optionally specify a keyboard shortcut and color highlight for it. Then click OK. Notice that the Record button is now active, letting you know that the application is watching. In this recording state, all the steps you perform (that are recordable) will be recorded and will start appearing under your new action in the palette.

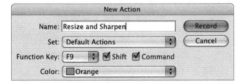

Figure 84b When creating a new action, you can choose an action set for it to be saved in, assign a function key combination, and select a highlight color for the action when it's in Button mode.

3. When you're finished adding steps to your action, click the Stop button at the bottom of the palette. With your action created, you can now run it on any open file or a batch of files (see #85).

Inserting the Nonrecordable

Some menu commands may not be recorded when creating an action, for instance, the Effects commands in Illustrator. Keep an eye on the Actions palette to see if the menu command you selected appears. If it doesn't, you may still be able to add it to your action. From the Actions palette menu, choose Insert Menu Item and then try selecting the menu command again.

#85 Batch Process Files in Photoshop and Illustrator

It's fairly easy in Photoshop or Illustrator to set up an action and perform it on a batch of files. Before you know it, hundreds of files will be processed without you even breaking a sweat.

To batch process a set of files, follow these steps:

1. In Photoshop, choose File > Automate > Batch. In Illustrator, choose Batch from the Actions palette menu.

2. In the Batch dialog (**Figure 85a**), select the action you want to use from the Set and Action menus to process your batch of files. The action along with the set it was saved in must be loaded into the Actions palette for it to be available in the Batch dialog.

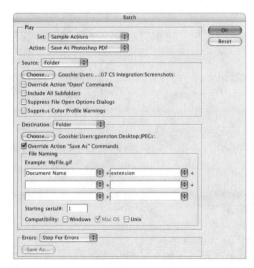

Figure 85a The Batch dialog might seem daunting at first, but it really isn't that bad if you break it down option by option. Just think of all the time it will save you.

3. For Source, click the Choose button to specify the folder location of the files to be processed. Photoshop offers a few other options besides Folder location that you can select from the Source menu. If you have a scanner or digital camera import plug-in, you can select the Import option as a source. Select the Opened Files option to process all the files you have open, or if you have files selected in Bridge you'd like to process, select the Bridge option.

4. You can set some additional processing options in the Source area of the dialog. Select the Override Action "Open" Commands option if the action you selected includes an Open command that you'd like to replace with your selection of source files. Select the Include All Subfolders option if you want the Batch command to process any files that exist in other folders within your source folder. Photoshop offers two more options for skipping open options dialogs and color profile warnings.

5. From the Destination menu, select what the Batch command should do with the files after processing: None, Save and Close, or Folder. Selecting None keeps the files open for you to save afterwards. Save and Close saves any changes to the processed files as if you performed a Save (File > Save) and then closed them. Selecting the Folder option enables the Choose button so you can specify a location for your processed files to be saved. Photoshop lets you define your file naming convention when saving to a folder.

6. Again, if your action includes a Save As command, be sure to select the Override Action "Save As" Commands option so that the command in the action will be ignored and your chosen destination folder will be used instead. Illustrator also provides an override option for Export commands in your action (**Figure 85b**).

(continued on next page)

Optimizing for Batches

For better performance when batch processing files in Photoshop, turn off the Automatically Create First Snapshot option in the History Options of the History palette menu and reduce the number of saved history states in the application's General Preferences.

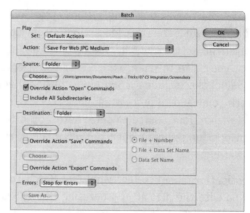

Figure 85b
Illustrator's
Batch dialog is a
kissing cousin to
Photoshop's. They
both include the
same core set of
options.

7. On the Errors menu, you can choose how the Batch command should handle any errors that occur; choose to either stop processing the files or continue processing and just log the errors.

8. Click OK and the Batch command goes to work, processing your files as fast as your system can manage it while you sit back and relax. Now that's automation.

#86 Batch Rename Files in Bridge

Many of the images we retrieve from our digital cameras are named with incredibly descriptive titles such as IMG_1899.JPG. And yes, you could argue that filenames really aren't as important as they once were since we can now rely on Bridge to actually show us the image files to select from. But still, you may want to better name your image files for those situations where Bridge may not be available to you or others dealing with your files. Funny enough, Bridge can actually help you batch rename multiple files for those times when Bridge isn't available.

Here's how to quickly batch rename files in Bridge:

1. Select the files you want to rename from the main area or by using the Folders pane. Selecting folders from within the Folders pane inherently selects the folder's contents.

2. Choose Tools > Batch Rename or use the keyboard shortcut: Shift+Command+R (Mac) or Shift+Control+R (Windows).

3. In the Batch Rename dialog (**Figure 86**), select the destination of your renamed files. You can choose to keep the renamed files in the same folder or copy or move them to a different folder. Click the Browse button and choose a destination if you opt to copy or move your renamed files to a different folder.

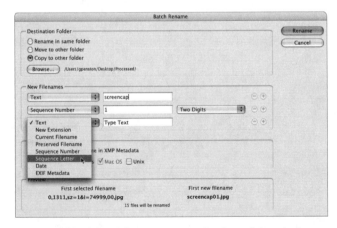

Figure 86 Bridge's Batch Rename command makes quick work of your file naming needs. It offers a set of useful options to help specify how your files should be named.

(continued on next page)

Applying Keywords

Since Bridge is a brand-new application to the suite, you may not know that it includes the ability to add keywords to files. Keywords allow you to easily find files later on by just searching on that keyword. To assign a keyword to selected files in Bridge, switch to the Keywords panel (it's grouped with the Metadata panel in the lower-left corner of the Bridge window by default). Just check any of the keywords you'd like to assign. You can add your own keywords by clicking the New Keyword button at the bottom of the panel. Once keywords are assigned to your files, you can use the Find command in Bridge to quickly locate them.

4. In the New Filenames area of the dialog, select options from the element menus or enter text to construct your file-renaming scheme. Click the plus or minus buttons to add or subtract elements to your file naming scheme. You can then glance at the Preview area to see how the files will actually be renamed.

5. You have a couple of additional options to choose from the aptly named Options area of the dialog. Select any additional operating systems you'd like your filenames to be compatible with. Your current operating system is checked by default and can't be unchecked. If you'd like Bridge to preserve the original filename in the metadata, be sure to select the Preserve current filename in XMP Metadata option.

6. Click the Rename button to let Bridge loose on your inadequately named files. Next thing you know, you'll have all your files renamed just as you specified.

Creating a Contact Sheet in InDesign via Bridge

#87

Sure, it's been possible for quite some time to create a contact sheet of your images in Photoshop. But with CS2, you can create a contact sheet in InDesign via Bridge. Choosing Bridge to generate your contact sheets in InDesign offers some compelling benefits over using Photoshop. For one, you can select an InDesign template, which could include your company's logo and contact information as the basis of the contact sheet. Since it's InDesign, your contact sheet can spill over to multiple pages as opposed to separate documents in Photoshop. Also, the generated contact sheet in InDesign links to the images instead of flattening them into a layer, letting you edit an image and have it update within the contact sheet.

Here's how to create a contact sheet in InDesign from Bridge:

1. In Bridge, select the images you want to include in your contact sheet. Note that the automated script that produces the contact sheet, is smart enough to create a new page when one fills up, so select as many images as you'd like.

2. Still in Bridge, choose Tools > InDesign > Create InDesign Contact Sheet. The Contact Sheet dialog opens (**Figure 87a**).

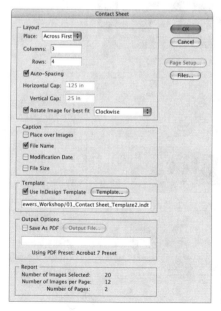

Figure 87a Bridge's contact sheet automation script for InDesign really shows off the scripting capabilities of Adobe CS2.

(continued on next page)

Using a Template for Your Contact Sheet

You can create an InDesign template as a basis for your contact sheet. This allows you to easily include details such as your company logo, contact information, disclaimer, page numbers, and so forth on each page. Add the details you want to appear on the main master page (see #41) of your document, making sure they appear outside the page margins. Save the document as a template by choosing File > Save As and selecting InDesign CS2 Template from the Format menu in the Save dialog. You can then use this template file when creating contact sheets.

3. From the Contact Sheet dialog, you can adjust the layout options, select the information that will appear in the caption under each image, and decide whether to use an InDesign Template (see the sidebar "Using a Template for Your Contact Sheet"). You can also choose to have the automated script save the contact sheet as a PDF once it's generated.

4. If you decide not to use an InDesign template, click the available Page Setup button to specify the page size and margins of your contact sheet.

5. You can optionally click the Files button to reorder your images or filter by file type those images that will be included in the contact sheet.

6. When you've finished adjusting the options, click OK and Bridge will automatically hand off the instructions to InDesign to start laying out your selected images into a multi-page contact sheet (**Figure 87b**).

Figure 87b After the contact sheet is complete, you can continue to work with the InDesign file just as any other. Contact sheets in InDesign have a leg up on the ones in Photoshop since you can use a template as your basis.

#88 Exploring Scripts in InDesign

InDesign is a page layout application laden with powerful features and tools. But if there happens to be a task you wish InDesign could help with, look no further than scripts. Scripts in InDesign are plain text files that can be written in AppleScript for Mac, VBScript for Windows, or JavaScript for cross-platform support to extend InDesign's base functionality to accomplish particular tasks faster or more efficiently.

Fortunately, you don't have to learn to code to reap the benefits of InDesign scripts. You can install scripts into InDesign that others have been so kind to develop and start running them with a simple double-click. Many sample scripts are available to you on the CS2 install disc. If you own Adobe Creative Suite 2 Premium, look on the Resources and extras disc (not Disk 2) and follow this path: Technical Information/InDesign CS2/Scripting/Adobe Sample Scripts/JavaScript. To install these sample scripts into InDesign, select all the scripts and copy them into your InDesign's Scripts folder (Adobe InDesign/Presets/Scripts). You should also copy the Read Me PDF found in the Adobe Sample Scripts folder to learn what each script does. Then quit InDesign if you happen to have it running. Launch InDesign and choose Window > Automation > Scripts to open the Scripts palette. The sample scripts you installed should now be available to you from this palette (**Figure 88**). To run a script, simply double-click it. Many of the scripts require you to have an object selected first, but they display a message window informing you of such.

Figure 88 Once you've loaded the sample scripts into InDesign, you'll have unleashed a whole new set of features and functionality that was lurking underneath the power of scripting.

(continued on next page)

Be sure to try each script to become familiar with its capabilities. For even more scripts, go to Adobe's Resource Center Studio Exchange at http://share.studio.adobe.com. Here you'll not only find scripts for InDesign and other CS2 applications, but other helpful tools such as templates and plug-ins. When I last checked, there were close to 200 scripts available for InDesign.

#89 Detecting Rollover Images in GoLive

One of the timesaving features in GoLive is its ability to detect rollover images by looking for commonly used suffixes to filenames such as "-out, -over, -down" when you add the main graphic to a page. For instance, if you created a graphic named "about.gif" and named the over and down states "about-over.gif" and "about-down.gif," GoLive will automatically associate the images to the main graphic in the Rollovers palette and produce the necessary code to string all the rollover states together, including efficient preloader code.

GoLive's Detect Rollover Images feature is on by default. So to take advantage of it, you just need to make sure GoLive is aware of your file naming conventions and that you save all your images in the same folder. To review GoLive detection settings, open the Rollovers palette (Window > Rollovers) and choose Rollover Detection Settings from the palette's menu. This actually brings up the Rollover settings in GoLive's Preferences dialog (**Figure 89a**). You can choose to follow any of the naming conventions shown or add your own naming scheme by clicking the New Item button 🔲. Click OK when you've finished reviewing the detection settings.

Keeping Rollovers Smart with ImageReady

ImageReady excels at helping you create button graphics with rollover states. What's more, GoLive and ImageReady work really well together. So instead of saving your optimized graphics in ImageReady, add your ImageReady file as a Photoshop Smart Object to your GoLive site with your rollover states assigned. When you add the Smart Object to a page in GoLive, your rollover states are still automatically detected, and you gain the flexibility to quickly make changes to the ImageReady file.

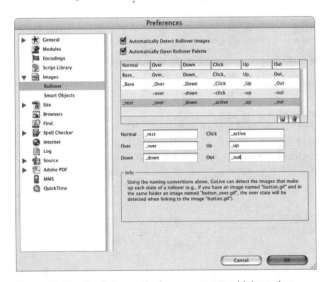

Figure 89a Use the Rollovers Preferences to see which naming conventions GoLive is set to detect, or add your own.

Now create and save all your rollover graphics to a folder within your GoLive site, using a naming convention GoLive is aware of. Drag your main graphic of the rollover set into a GoLive page. A small rollover icon 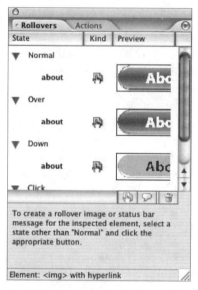 appears in the lower-left corner of your graphic, letting you know that GoLive has detected your rollover states. Go to the Rollovers palette, and you'll see that all your rollover states have been automatically created (**Figure 89b**). Switch to Preview mode to see your rollovers in action.

Figure 89b Once you've added your main graphic, GoLive intelligently detects the other rollover images in the set and then builds the entire rollover interaction for you in the Rollovers palette.

#90 Converting Multiple Documents in GoLive

If you have an old site with hundreds of pages that you want to convert to XHTML, you may be discouraged thinking it will be a long tiresome job. GoLive actually automates the process of converting documents of this nature so that it's relatively quick and painless.

You can find a handful of document conversion options in GoLive by choosing Special > Convert (**Figure 90a**):

Converting Your Working Document

You can more readily convert your working document's language, doctype, and markup (HTML/XHTML) using the fly-out menu located in the top-right corner of the document window.

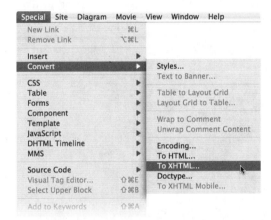

Figure 90a The Convert option is your ticket to all the document conversion options GoLive offers.

- **Encoding:** Changes the selected character set (charset) within your documents.

- **To HTML:** Converts your XHTML documents to HTML.

- **To XHTML:** Converts your HTML documents to XHTML.

- **Doctype:** Allows you to choose a different DOCTYPE for your documents. The DOCTYPE of your document informs browsers of how compliant your code is (transitional vs. strict). If you want to convert from HTML Transitional to XHTML Transitional, you'll need to use the To XHTML option.

- **To XHTML Mobile:** Converts the document or documents you've selected in your site so they're ready for XHTML Mobile.

(continued on next page)

Each conversion option opens its own dialog. Here you adjust any settings and decide which documents to run the conversion on. Except for XHTML Mobile, you can specify which documents in your site to perform the conversion on by clicking the Work On pop-up menu (**Figure 90b**). You can choose to convert only the document you're working on (top document), a selection of documents, all the documents within your site, or a set of documents based on a query.

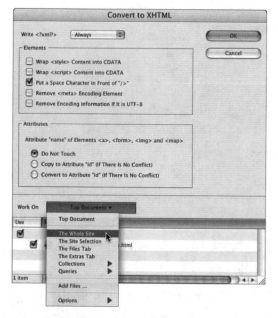

Figure 90b Use the Work On pop-up menu to specify which files you want GoLive to convert. Your selection list appears directly below the menu.

When you're ready to convert your selection of documents, click OK. Depending on the number of documents you've selected and the speed of your computer, the conversion process may take a while. This may be an opportune time for a cup of coffee. But when you return, your documents should all be converted, saving you countless hours of coding.

CHAPTER TEN

Working with Versions and Reviews

It's odd that creative tools have evolved through the years without addressing two critical points in the creative process: managing versions and setting up reviews. In this information age, our team members and clients are no longer working beside us or down the street but rather on the other side of the country or in another country altogether.

Thankfully, Adobe has recognized the need for tools to help us work more collaboratively with our team and our clients regardless of whether or not they're in the same office. Adobe CS2 Premium includes Acrobat 7 Professional, the de facto standard when it comes to working with PDF documents. Whether you need to start a review, add comments, or make minor edits to a PDF, Acrobat is the application to reach for. Also in CS2 is a brand-new edition of Adobe's versioning and workflow management tool, Version Cue CS2. Version Cue CS2 offers a robust set of features and tight integration throughout the suite along with the ability to view and manage your versions via Adobe Bridge.

In this chapter, I intend to highlight ways you can use these two powerful tools to help you explore different directions in your designs and manage those inevitable changes as well as help you set up PDF reviews and work with the comments you receive in them.

#91 Working with Version Cue Versions

Using the Adobe Dialog

Always use the Adobe dialog states (or Bridge) when opening, saving, placing, importing, and exporting files. The Adobe dialog offers a much richer experience than your OS dialogs for working with Version Cue projects, providing you with direct navigation to your Version Cue projects and important information regarding the files such as status, version comments, and if alternates are available.

Version Cue versions are historical snapshots of your files that you decide to capture and save when you've made enough edits or changes to your file to warrant a new version. Once you've set up Version Cue (see #15), created your projects, and started saving versions within it (see #16), you may want to dig a little deeper and learn how to work with Version Cue versions.

When you open a Version Cue project file, a working copy is created on your local hard drive. The file is then marked as "In Use" to prevent other users from opening the file and accidentally overwriting any of your changes. That isn't to say that your other team members are totally locked out of using the file. Depending on how the Version Cue project is set up (see #94), they may be able to open the file but will be required to save their changes as a separate version. An alert appears (**Figure 91a**) when you attempt to open a file that is in use by someone else on your team. You have the option of closing the document and waiting for that person to finish making changes or continuing to work with the file at the risk of having to manually reconcile any differences between each other's work.

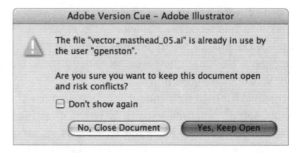

Figure 91a When opening a file that's already open by someone else in the Version Cue Workspace, an alert appears giving you the option of continuing to work on the file or not.

Once you're through editing the file, you can save a new version by choosing File > Save a Version. This saves the file to the Version Cue Workspace and marks the status of the files "Synchronized," meaning your working copy and the file in the Version Cue project are identical.

You can view and manage the version of a file from the Versions dialog, which you can access by selecting Versions from a myriad of menus available throughout CS2: the Project Tools menu 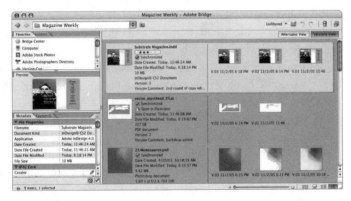 in the Adobe dialog state of a CS2 application's file dialogs; the document status menu in Photoshop, Illustrator, and InDesign when the file is open; and the contextual menu when selecting the original file in any view of Bridge. Switch to the Versions and Alternates view in Bridge to view all the versions of the files in a folder at once (**Figure 91b**). You can also perform version status updates directly from Bridge. When a file is selected in Bridge, commands to synchronize, mark a file as in use, or revert a file to its last version are available by choosing Tools > Version Cue.

Figure 91b The Versions and Alternates view in Bridge makes it easy to visualize and manage the versions in your project.

#92 Creating Version Cue Alternates

If you've made dramatic changes to a version, you may want to consider saving it as a Version Cue alternate. Alternates let you explore an entirely different design direction for a project while keeping an association to the document version it was based on. This is just one of the ways you can use alternates. You can also create an alternate for different languages or regions a document may need to address. Multiple alternates can be created, all pointing back to the same version. These are referred to as alternate groups. If that's unclear, try thinking about alternates as different renditions based on the same document whereas versions are historical snapshots of changes made to a document. Alternates give you the flexibility to create different design directions or renditions and work with them in the Creative Suite applications. Note that Acrobat doesn't support alternates.

In order to create an alternate of a file that you're working on, you must first save or copy it into your Version Cue Workspace. Using Bridge, click Version Cue in the Favorites pane to navigate to the Version Cue project you saved the file in. Double-click the versioned file to open it in the CS2 application that it was created with. With the file open, you can now take the design in a completely different direction.

When you're ready to save your work as an alternate, choose File > Save As. If you're not in the Adobe dialog state, click the Use Adobe Dialog button to get there. In the Save As dialog, select the Save As Alternate option located at the bottom of the dialog (**Figure 92**).

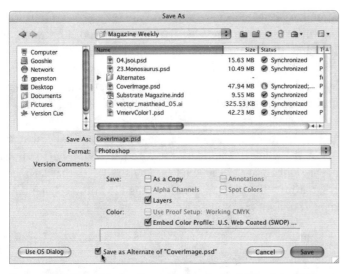

Figure 92 Select the Save as Alternate option in the Adobe dialog to save an open file as an alternate.

If you'd like to keep the same file name as your original file, save the alternate to a different folder. You can save the alternate to the same folder as the original but you need to use a different name. Unlike versions in Version Cue, alternates appear as separate files in your project. This is why I suggest storing all your alternates in another folder. Also, a file can only be a part of one alternate group at a time, and alternates cannot span multiple projects.

#93 Working with Version Cue Alternates

Other Uses for Alternates

The obvious use for alternates is to take a file in a different design direction or just explore another direction, but there are plenty of other uses for alternates. You can use them to define a set of files that use different languages or cater to different regions of the country. You can also use them for editions of a file for different printing formats, such as low- versus high-resolution or one- color versus four-color.

After you've created your alternates (see #92), you can start working with them in Bridge as well as in Photoshop, Illustrator, and InDesign. Use Bridge to view and manage any alternates you have associated with your files. Then take advantage of using alternates by easily swapping a placed alternate with another file in the alternate group directly within one of the major CS2 applications.

To view alternates of a file in Bridge, switch to the Versions and Alternates view ⊞ using the icon in the lower-right corner of the window. Then click the Alternates View button in the upper-right corner of the window. Any alternates that have been created for a file will appear beside the file in the column on the right (**Figure 93a**).

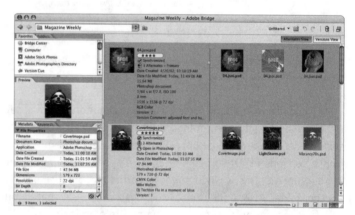

Figure 93a Use the Versions and Alternates view in Bridge to see your alternate groups. You can also drag files into the alternates column of this view to make them alternates.

If you have an alternate group (multiple alternates to a file), the primary alternate filename will be boldfaced. A primary alternate provides a way for you to mark one of the alternates as your preferred or possibly approved alternative direction. You can make any alternate the primary alternate by Control-clicking (Mac) or right-clicking (Windows) it while in the Versions and Alternates view and then choosing Primary Alternate from the contextual menu. Then you or others working with you will know which alternate to use first when opening in Photoshop or placing in Illustrator or InDesign.

If a file is part of an alternate group, a small Alternates icon appears next to the file name in Bridge, the Adobe dialog state in the Alternates column, and in the Links palette in Illustrator and InDesign (**Figure 93b**). If the file happens to be the primary alternate, the Primary Alternate icon appears instead.

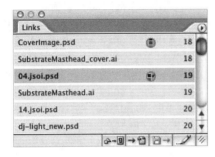

Figure 93b Linked files that happen to be alternates are indicated by these little icons in the Links palettes of Illustrator and InDesign.

In Illustrator or InDesign you can place a file that belongs to an alternate group just as you would any other file. Once placed, you can quickly swap the file with one of the available alternates by selecting the file in the Links palette and choosing Alternates from the palette's menu. In the Alternates dialog (**Figure 93c**), select the alternate you want to use and click the Relink button. Now when your clients call to tell you they prefer the "blue one" instead, you can update your files before you're even off the phone with them.

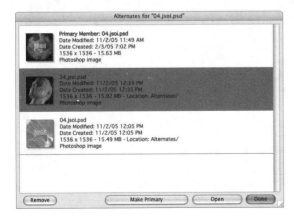

Figure 93c The Alternates dialog allows you to view alternates of a file when you're not in Bridge.

#93: Working with Version Cue Alternates

#94 Exploring the Version Cue Administration Utility

Although much of what you use Version Cue for can be accomplished through Bridge and the other CS2 applications, you may need to open the Version Cue Administration utility to complete some of the more advanced tasks that can't be done elsewhere. The utility is meant to accomplish the more administrative-related tasks, such as managing users and their project privileges, starting a Web-based PDF review, or backing up Version Cue projects. All are very helpful features that you may be interested in, depending on how much you embrace Version Cue in your creative workflow.

The Version Cue Administration utility is accessed via your browser. To load the utility, select Advanced Administration from the Version Cue menu (Mac) or the Version Cue system tray icon (Windows) (see #15). The Administration login page opens in your browser. When the Creative Suite is first installed, Version Cue creates a default user login with administrator privileges. Enter "system/" as the login as well as the password. Then click the Login button.

Once you've successfully logged into the Administration utility, you'll be taken to the Administration window (**Figure 94a**). Here's what you'll find:

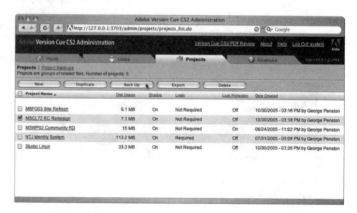

Figure 94a Although you can use Version Cue without ever launching the Administration utility, you may want to use this utility for more advanced control over users and projects.

- The **Home tab**. This tab offers links to common administrative tasks, such as adding and editing users, removing old versions, and creating new projects.

- The **Users tab** allows you to add new users to Version Cue and easily assign them an access level and project specific privileges (**Figure 94b**).

- From the **Projects tab**, you can create new projects and manage existing projects. You can also see how much disk space each project is using up and choose to back them up from here (see #95).

- The **Advanced tab** includes tools for importing Version Cue 1.0 data, setting preferences for Version Cue, backing up the entire Version Cue Workspace, and accessing logs and reports.

Just above the Advanced tab is the Version Cue CS2 PDF Review link. Clicking this link directs you to the Review area of the utility so you can create a Web-based PDF review (see #96).

Figure 94b The Users page lets you add additional members to your Version Cue and assign them limited or unrestricted privileges over each project.

#94: Exploring the Version Cue Administration Utility

#95 Backing Up Your Version Cue Projects

Scheduling Project Backups

Using the Version Cue Administration utility you can schedule recurring backups of your projects. In the Projects tab, click a project you want to schedule for a backup. Then on the Project's Properties page, click the New button in the Backup Configurations panel. Specify a configuration name and the schedule for how often you want the backup to run as well as how many backups to be stored.

Another convenient feature introduced with Version Cue CS2 is the ability to back up all the information in your Version Cue projects using the Administration utility. As you start to rely on Version Cue more and more to manage your project files and their versions, you'll want to be sure to keep backups in case of any hardware failures or to archive completed projects.

Here's how to back up your Version Cue projects:

1. Log into the Version Cue Administration utility (see #94).

2. Click the Projects tab. In the Projects list, select the check box next to the project you want to back up and then click Back Up (**Figure 95a**). (You can only select one project at a time to back up.)

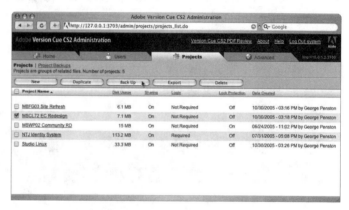

Figure 95a Go to the Projects tab to select the project you want to back up.

3. On the page that appears, decide on the details of your backup (**Figure 95b**). You can choose to keep the suggested backup name or enter a new one. Uncheck any of the project components you'd like to omit. Files are always backed up so this option can't be unchecked. Project File Versions backs up all the versions of the files; Project Metadata backs up the information embedded in your documents by CS2; and Users/ User Assignments backs up information about the users and their privileges for the project. Enter any comments you'd like to add about the project backup in the Comments box.

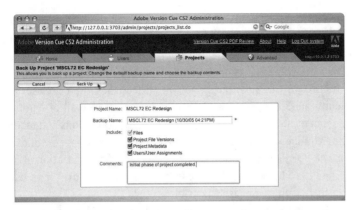

Figure 95b From this screen, you can choose which parts of the project data are backed up and add a descriptive comment that may help you later when you need to restore a project.

4. Click the Back Up button in the header bar. Once the backup is complete, a confirmation page appears displaying all the details of your backup. By default, project backups are stored in a folder titled "Backups" on the file system where you have Version Cue being served. You can change this backup storage location to another hard drive or network drive using the Version Cue CS2 Control Panel in the Locations tab.

You can access all your backups from the Project Backups link in the Projects tab. If you want to restore a backup, select it from this list and click Save.

> **Note:** You'll need System Administrator privileges to restore a project backup. Otherwise, the project names will be visible but not have check boxes to select them.

Backing Up Your Entire Workspace

You can back up your entire Version Cue Workspace, which includes all your project, files, and versions, by clicking the Advanced tab in the Version Cue Administration utility. From the Advanced page, click Back Up Version Cue Data in the Maintenance Section. Since this will back up every file and version in your workspace, be sure your destination can handle what typically can be a large amount of data.

#96 Initiating a Version Cue PDF Review

Enabling Version Cue in Acrobat

With CS2, all applications in the suite have Version Cue enabled by default—well, except for Acrobat. To switch on Version Cue in Acrobat 7, select Enable Version Cue Workflow file management in the application's preferences in the General section.

New in Version Cue CS2 is the ability to create and conduct a Web-based review of any PDF documents in your Version Cue Workspace. You set up the review in the Version Cue Administration utility and then invite participants via email. Invited participants then click the link in the email message, which launches their browser and loads the PDF for review. From there, they can use all of Acrobat's commenting and markup tools to express their opinions and request any changes. All the comments that are sent back are consolidated in the PDF Review section of the Version Cue Administration utility. Since the PDF review is Web-based, it's ideal for those times when an in-person review isn't possible.

Follow these steps to create a Version Cue PDF review:

1. Save your PDF for review in the Version Cue Workspace. You can accomplish this by either enabling Version Cue in Acrobat (see the sidebar "Enabling Version Cue in Acrobat") and saving a version to one of your projects or by using Bridge to copy the PDF from your local hard drive to a project in the Version Cue Workspace.

2. Launch the Version Cue Administration utility and log in (see #94).

3. Click the Version Cue CS2 PDF Review link located in the upper-right portion of the screen. This takes you to the PDF Review area of the utility.

4. Click the Start a Review link on the Home page. This delivers you to the Document List page where all the PDF documents in your Version Cue Workspace are listed (**Figure 96a**). Since native Illustrator files (ai) are PDF compatible, you'll see these listed as well. You can filter the document list using the controls located above the list.

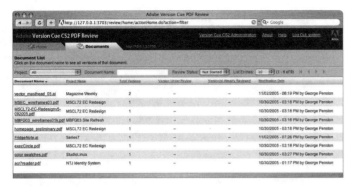

Figure 96a The Document List in the PDF Review area of the Administration utility makes available all the PDF documents in your Version Cue Workspace.

5. Click the name of the file you want to use in the review. The next page displays the versions of the PDF, if any exist. Select the radio button next to the version you want to use in the review, and then click the Start Review button above the versions list.

6. On the next screen, you can specify a deadline for the review and whether it should be an open or private review (**Figure 96b**). Open reviews allow reviewers to see each other's comments, whereas private reviews limit them to viewing only their own comments. Deselect any of the users in your workspace you don't want to include in the review.

(continued on next page)

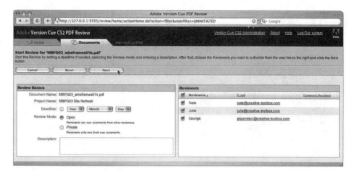

Figure 96b From this screen, you can choose a deadline for the review, whether or not reviewers can see each other's comments, and who the reviewers are.

7. Click Next and the last screen appears. From here, you can customize the subject and message that will show up in the email invitation. You can choose not to send an email invitation, but then reviewers may not know to check their reviews in the Administration utility.

8. Your default mail client will open with the email invitation ready for you to send.

When the recipients receive the invitation, they simply click the link in the email. Version Cue then delivers the PDF file to their browser for them to review. They then use the commenting tools available in the Acrobat browser plug-in to add any comments and notes. Once they click the Send/Receive Comments button, the comments are uploaded to the Version Cue Workspace where all the comments are consolidated.

> **Note:** The Acrobat browser plug-in must be loaded in the reviewer's browser to properly support the PDF review. Mac users must explicitly set this in Acrobat's preferences if Safari is set to handle PDF viewing.

#97 Touching Up PDFs in Acrobat

Let's say you just finished exporting an overly complex InDesign file as a PDF to prepare it for a review that's supposed to happen in 10 minutes. You have the PDF open in Acrobat when you notice a major typo staring back at you. You might think all is lost since you don't have enough time to go back and export the entire PDF into InDesign. But don't despair, Acrobat's smart set of TouchUp tools are there to help.

The TouchUp Text and Object tools permit you to make last minute, minor edits to your PDF documents directly within Acrobat (**Figure 97a**). The tools work much like you would expect in an Adobe application. You can call on these powerful tools by choosing Tools > Advanced Editing > Show TouchUp Toolbar within Acrobat. Note that if the document has certain security settings applied, you may not be able to touch it up.

Touching Up the Reading Order

One other tool in the TouchUp toolbar is the TouchUp Reading Order tool. This tool helps you adjust the reading order of your document to make it accessible for vision- or motor-impaired users.

Figure 97a The TouchUp tools in Acrobat make it easy to perform last minute corrections or edits to your PDF documents.

(continued on next page)

You can select, edit, and even format text with the TouchUp Text tool 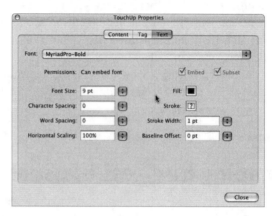. To make text changes, select the TouchUp Text tool and then select your text. To edit the text properties of the text you have selected, Control-click (Mac) or right-click (Windows) and choose Properties from the contextual menu. The TouchUp Properties window (**Figure 97b**) opens, allowing you to change several formatting properties of the selected text.

Figure 97b The TouchUp Properties window allows you to adjust the more popular formatting properties.

The TouchUp Object tool allows you to select objects to reposition or delete them. You can also edit just the object in Photoshop or Illustrator. To edit an object you have selected with the tool, Control-click (Mac) or right-click (Windows) and choose either Edit Object or Edit Image. Only one of these options will be available depending on the type of object you have selected. Once you've made your edits in Photoshop or Illustrator, you can place the artwork directly back into the PDF.

#98 Setting Up an Email-based PDF Review in Acrobat

If you and your clients tend to work better by communicating by email or you are unable to or prefer not to host your PDF review online (see #96), consider initiating an email-based PDF review instead. Acrobat 7 Professional makes it easy to conduct a PDF review via email. Email-based reviews have advantages over just attaching a PDF to an email message, such as being able to include Adobe Reader users in the review process and the ability to automatically merge all the reviewer's comments into a single document (see #100).

Follow these steps to set up an email-based review in Acrobat:

1. Open your PDF file in Acrobat and choose Comments > Send for Review > Send by Email for Review. If you haven't supplied Acrobat with your email address, you'll be prompted to enter it in the Identity Setup dialog. Enter your email address along with any other information you want to include and click Complete.

2. In Step 1 of the Send by Email for Review dialog, your open PDF should be specified in the menu. From here you can choose a different PDF for review. If everything looks good, click Next.

3. In Step 2 of the review setup, choose the people you'd like to invite to participate in the review (**Figure 98a**). You can either enter email addresses directly in the box or select them from your saved addresses by clicking the Address Book button. Click Next to proceed to the last step.

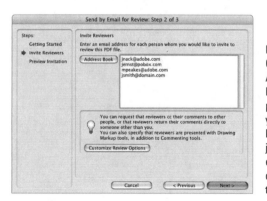

Figure 98a Click the Address Book button to select people from your address book to invite or just type their email addresses directly into the box.

(continued on next page)

Sizing for Email Delivery

If your review PDF is over 5 MB, you'll be asked if it's okay to proceed with the review setup. Many mail systems do not allow email attachments over 5 MB (although some allow as much as 20 MB). If you're concerned that your PDF won't get through, click No and exit the review setup. Try using the PDF Optimizer (Advanced > PDF Optimizer) to reduce your PDF to an email-friendly file size.

Customizing Your Review Options

Click the Customize Review Options button in the second step of the review setup if you'd like to enable the drawing markup tools for review. You can also request that reviewers return their comments to other email addresses as well or an address other than your own. Also by default, users of the free Adobe Reader 7 will be able to participate in the review. This option unlocks the commenting features in Adobe Reader but adds some limits to the commenting features in Acrobat. Deselect this option if you want to limit the review to only users of Acrobat.

4. In Step 3, preview the email subject and message that will be sent to the reviewers you invited (**Figure 98b**). If you want to make any additions or changes to the invitation, you can do so by typing over the default text. But keep in mind that the message includes instructions for your recipients on how to participate in the review. When you're ready to send the invitation, click Send Invitation. Acrobat then creates the email invitation with your PDF file attached and sends it out for review.

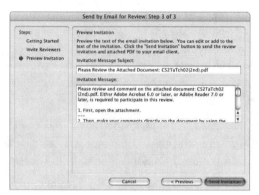

Figure 98b In this final step, you can preview and make any edits to the subject and message of the email invitation that will be sent to the people you've invited.

#99 Adding Comments in Acrobat

Acrobat serves up a complete set of commenting and markup tools for you to communicate your thoughts and edits when reviewing a PDF document. Comments can take the form of notes, stamps, highlighting of elements, and other types of markups for indicating text edits, such as strikethroughs for deletion. All of these tools are grouped together in the Commenting toolbar. In a review workflow these tools automatically appear, but you can access them at any time by choosing View > Toolbars > Commenting.

Here's a brief overview of the tools available in the Commenting toolbar and what they are used for:

- **Note tool:** This is probably the most common tool used for commenting. With the tool selected, click or draw a box near or on the portion of the PDF you want to add a note comment to (think sticky notes for PDFs). Using the Select tool ⌶▸, you can reposition the note icon so that the note comment points to the area of interest.

- **Indicate Text Edits tools:** Use these tools to edit text in the document. To indicate text that should be inserted, click between words or characters and start typing. To show where text should be deleted, select the text and then press the Delete or Backspace key. To indicate that text should be replaced, select the text and start typing over it.

- **Stamp tools:** Use these tools much like you would their real world counterparts. Stamp a PDF to mark a document confidential or to indicate you have reviewed it. Click and hold on the Stamp tools icon to choose from the variety of preset stamps available. There are even dynamic stamps such as a name stamp and a time stamp. Once you've selected a stamp, click anywhere on the PDF to apply it.

(continued on next page)

Commenting in Adobe Reader 7

It's now possible to enable the commenting and markup tools in the free Adobe Reader 7, so just about anyone can collaborate in a PDF review. This option is on by default when starting an email-based review (see #98), but you can also turn this option on at any time in an open PDF in Acrobat by choosing Comments > Enable for Commenting in Adobe Reader. Then anyone who opens the PDF in Adobe Reader will have many of the same commenting tools available as those found in Acrobat.

Highlighter tools: The Highlighter tools include the High-lighter Text tool, the Cross-Out Text tool, and the Underline Text tool. Click and hold on the small arrow beside the High-lighter tools icon to choose the appropriate tool. Select text with any of these tools to call attention to it. You can then double-click the highlighted text to add a note.

Attach a File as a Comment tools: You can add a file or audio attachment using these tools. These comments are tracked in the review workflow like other comments and appear in the Comment List (Comments > Show Comments List). They will also appear in the Attachments tab along with the number of the page to which they were attached.

#100 Collecting Comments from a PDF Review

Once you've started an email-based PDF review (see #98) and have begun to receive comments, you may wonder how you're ever going to consolidate all the feedback from the various reviewers. Well, you needn't worry: Acrobat takes care of all this for you. When you open the PDF document containing comments, Acrobat recognizes if it's part of a tracked review and offers you the option of merging the comments.

When you receive an email with an attached PDF with comments, double-click the attachment to open it in Acrobat. Acrobat will automatically identify the document as part of the review being tracked and will display a dialog asking you whether or not you'd like to merge the comments (**Figure 100**).

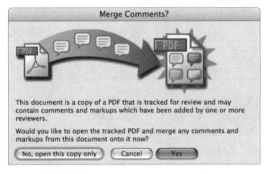

Figure 100 The Merge Comments dialog asks if you want to integrate the review copy comments into the original PDF. The illustration attempts to communicate what's going to happen.

In the Merge Comments dialog, click Yes to have Acrobat open the original PDF and incorporate the comments from the reviewed copy. You also have the option of opening the copy directly or canceling the merge action altogether. Continue to collect the comments in the original PDF as you receive all the replies to the review. Once you've collected all the feedback, you can easily print the consolidated comments along with the original document by choosing File > Print with Comments Summary.

Tracking Your Reviews

To keep track of the status and comments of your PDF reviews in Acrobat use the Tracker. To access the Tracker, choose Comments > Tracker. This window lists all of your reviews and pertinent details along with who's provided feedback and who hasn't. You can even send email reminders or invite additional people to a selected review using the Manage button menu.

Index

Peachpit
Essential books for the creative community

Visit Peachpit on the Web at www.peachpit.com

- Read the latest articles and download timesaving tipsheets from best-selling authors such as Scott Kelby, Robin Williams, Lynda Weinman, Ted Landau, and more!

- Join the Peachpit Club and save 25% off all your online purchases at peachpit.com every time you shop—plus enjoy free UPS ground shipping within the United States.

- Search through our entire collection of new and upcoming titles by author, ISBN, title, or topic. There's no easier way to find just the book you need.

- Sign up for newsletters offering special Peachpit savings and new book announcements so you're always the first to know about our newest books and killer deals.

- Did you know that Peachpit also publishes books by Apple, New Riders, Adobe Press, Macromedia Press and palmOne Press? Swing by the Peachpit family section of the site and learn about all our partners and series.

- Got a great idea for a book? Check out our About section to find out how to submit a proposal. You could write our next best-seller!

You'll find all this and more at www.peachpit.com. Stop by and take a look today!